STILL STEAMING

A Guide to Britain's Standard Gauge Steam Railways 2012-2013

EDITOR
John Robinson

Sixteenth Edition

RAILWAY LOCATOR MAP

The numbers shown on this map relate to the page numbers for each railway. Pages 5-6 contain an alphabetical listing of the railways featured in this guide. Please note that the markers on this map show the approximate location only.

FOREWORD & ACKNOWLEDGEMENTS

We were greatly impressed by the friendly and cooperative manner of the staff and helpers of the railways which we selected to appear in this book, and wish to thank them all for the help they have given. In addition we wish to thank Bob Budd (cover design) and Michael Robinson (page layouts) for their help and also Jonathan James who has provided us with photographs for several railways.

Although we believe that the information contained in this guide is accurate at the time of going to press, we, and the Railways and Museums itemised, are unable to accept liability for any loss, damage, distress or injury suffered as a result of any inaccuracies. Furthermore, we and the Railways are unable to guarantee operating and opening times which may always be subject to cancellation without notice.

We realise that other UK Standard Gauge railways are operating or about to resume operating (notably, the Eden Valley Railway and the Epping Ongar Railway), and we hope to include this in a future edition of Still Steaming.

If you feel we should include other locations or information in future editions, please let us know so that we may give them consideration. We would like to thank you for buying this guide and wish you 'Happy Steaming'!

John Robinson

EDITOR

Note: Further copies of our railway guides Still Steaming, Little Puffers and Tiny Trains may be obtained, post free, from our address below or ordered on-line via our web site – www.stillsteaming.com

British Library Cataloguing in Publication Data
A catalogue record for this book is available from the British Library

ISBN-13: 978-1-86223-227-3

Copyright © 2012, MARKSMAN PUBLICATIONS. (01472 696226)
72 St. Peter's Avenue, Cleethorpes, N.E. Lincolnshire, DN35 8HU, England

Manufactured in the UK by T.J. International Ltd.

COVER PICTURE

The cover picture was kindly supplied by Brian Wakefield and shows loan locomotives about to leave Ludborough Station on the Lincolnshire Wolds Railway.

CONTENTS

ALDERNEY RAILWAY

Address: P.O. Box 75, Alderney, Channel Islands GY9 3DA	**Nº of Steam Locos**: None at present
Telephone Nº: None	**Nº of Other Locos**: 2
Year Formed: 1978	**Nº of Members**: 50
Location of Line: Braye Harbour to Mannez Quarry, Alderney	**Annual Membership Fee**: £15.00
	Approx Nº of Visitors P.A.: 2,000+
	Gauge: Standard
Length of Line: 2 miles	**Web site**: www.alderneyrailway.com

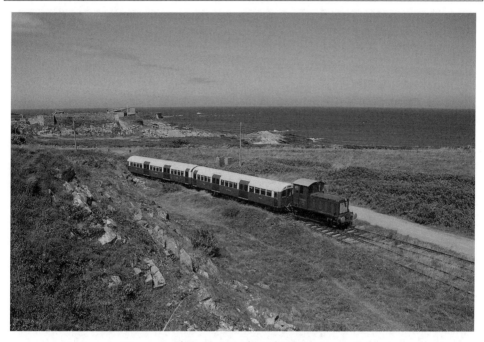

Photo courtesy of David Staines

GENERAL INFORMATION

Nearest Mainline Station: Not applicable
Nearest Bus Station: Not applicable
Car Parking: Available on site
Coach Parking: Available on site
Souvenir Shop(s): Yes
Food & Drinks: None at the Railway itself but available nearby

SPECIAL INFORMATION

The original line was built during the 1840s to assist in the construction of the large breakwater in Braye Harbour and fortifications on the island.
The line itself opened in 1847 and was the first nationalised railway run by the Admiralty.

OPERATING INFORMATION

Opening Times: Sundays and Bank Holidays from Easter until the September with a Santa Special also running in December. Trains usually run at 2.30pm and 3.30pm.
Steam Working: None at present
Prices: Adult Return £4.50
Child Return £3.00

Detailed Directions:
The Railway is situated adjacent to Braye Harbour.

APPLEBY FRODINGHAM R.P.S.

Address: Appleby Frodingham Railway Preservation Society, P.O. Box 1, Scunthorpe DN16 1BP **Telephone Nº**: (01652) 656661 **Year Formed**: 1990 **Location of Line**: Tata Steelworks, Scunthorpe	**Length of Line**: 15 miles used on tours from almost 100 miles of track **Nº of Steam Locos**: 2 **Nº of Other Locos**: 3 **Nº of Members**: 60 **Gauge**: Standard **Web site**: www.afrps.co.uk

GENERAL INFORMATION

Nearest Mainline Station: Scunthorpe (1 mile)
Nearest Bus Station: Scunthorpe (½ mile)
Car Parking: Large free car park at the site
Coach Parking: At the site
Souvenir Shop(s): Yes – at the Loco Shed
Food & Drinks: Available at the Loco Shed

SPECIAL INFORMATION

The Society operates 8 and 15 mile Rail and Brake Van tours of the Tata steelworks site (which covers almost 12 square miles) using its extensive internal railway system.

OPERATING INFORMATION

Opening Times: Selected weekends throughout the year which <u>must</u> be pre-booked via (01652) 657053 or e-mail – bookings@afrps.co.uk
Private Hire of a train is now available for parties and anniversaries with use of the Lounge coach.
Steam Working: Most active days. Ask for further details when booking.
Prices: Free – but the society relies on donations which are collected at the end of each tour.
Please note that children cannot be carried on Brake Van tours due to the open verandahs.

Detailed Directions by Car:
Exit the M180 at Junction 4 and take the A18 into Scunthorpe. Turn right at the roundabout by Morrisons supermarket and follow the road along for approximately ½ mile. Turn right into Entrance E. Car parking is available on the left and the path to the station is on the right.   SatNav users please enter: DN16 1XA

AVON VALLEY RAILWAY

Address: Bitton Station, Bath Road, Bitton, Bristol BS30 6HD	**Nº of Steam Locos:** 6
Telephone Nº: (0117) 932-5538	**Nº of Other Locos:** 5
Year Formed: 1973	**Nº of Members:** Approximately 700
Location of Line: Midway between Bristol and Bath on A431	**Annual Membership Fee:** £15.00
	Approx Nº of Visitors P.A.: 80,000
Length of Line: 3 miles	**Gauge:** Standard
	Web site: www.avonvalleyrailway.org
	E-mail: info@avonvalleyrailway.org

GENERAL INFORMATION

Nearest Mainline Station: Keynsham (1½ miles)
Nearest Bus Station: Bristol or Bath (7 miles)
Car Parking: Available at Bitton Station
Coach Parking: Available at Bitton Station
Souvenir Shop(s): Yes
Food & Drinks: Yes

SPECIAL INFORMATION

The line has been extended through the scenic Avon Valley towards Bath and a new platform is now open linking with walks along the River Avon and local Public Houses.

OPERATING INFORMATION

Opening Times: Every Sunday and some Saturdays from Easter to October and on weekends during December. Also Bank Holiday Mondays, Wednesdays in June and July and Tuesdays to Thursdays during School Holidays. Also open for Santa Specials over Christmas. Open 10.30am to 5.00pm.
Steam Working: 11.00am to 4.00pm
Prices: Adult £6.50
 Child £5.00
 Family Tickets £18.00
 Senior Citizens £5.50

Detailed Directions by Car:
From All Parts: Exit the M4 at Junction 18. Follow the A46 towards Bath and at the junction with the A420 turn right towards Bristol. At Bridge Yate turn left onto the A4175 and continue until you reach the A431. Turn right and Bitton Station is 100 yards on the right.

BARROW HILL ROUNDHOUSE RAILWAY CENTRE

Address: Barrow Hill Roundhouse, Campbell Drive, Barrow Hill, Staveley, Chesterfield   S43 2PR
Telephone N°: (01246) 472450
Year Formed: 1998
Location: Staveley, near Chesterfield
Length of Line: ¾ mile

N° of Steam Locos: 12
N° of Other Locos: Over 40
N° of Members: Approximately 400
Annual Membership Fee: £17.00 (Adult)
Approx N° of Visitors P.A.: 30,000
Gauge: Standard
Web site: www.barrowhill.org

GENERAL INFORMATION

Nearest Mainline Station:
Chesterfield (3½ miles)
Nearest Bus Station:
Chesterfield (3 miles)
Car Parking: Space available for 300 cars
Coach Parking: Available
Souvenir Shop(s): Yes
Food & Drinks: Yes – buffet

SPECIAL INFORMATION

Britain's last remaining operational railway roundhouse provides storage and repair facilities for standard gauge steam, diesel and electric locomotives.

OPERATING INFORMATION

Opening Times: Open at weekends throughout the year from 10.00am to 4.00pm.
Steam Working: Special open days only. 2012 dates – Steam Gala on 13th, 14th & 15th April; Rail Ale Festival on 18th & 19th May; Model Rail Live on 22nd & 23rd September; Santa Steam Trains on 15th and 16th December.
Please phone for further details or check the railway's web site.
Prices: Please phone for prices.

Detailed Directions by Car:
Exit the M1 at Junction 30 and take the A619 to Staveley (about 3½ miles). Pass through Staveley, turn right at Troughbrook onto 'Works Road'. Continue along for ¾ mile, pass under the railway bridge and take the turn immediately on the right. Turn left onto Campbell Drive and the Roundhouse is on the left. The railway is signposted with Brown Tourist signs.

THE BATTLEFIELD LINE

Address: The Battlefield Line, Shackerstone Station, Shackerstone, Warwickshire CV13 6NW
Telephone Nº: (01827) 880754
Year Formed: 1968
Location of Line: North West of Market Bosworth
Length of Line: 5 miles

Nº of Steam Locos: 5
Nº of Other Locos: 23
Nº of Members: 500 approximately
Annual Membership Fee: £15.00 Adult; £25.00 Family
Approx Nº of Visitors P.A.: 50,000
Gauge: Standard
Web site: www.battlefield-line-railway.co.uk

GENERAL INFORMATION

Nearest Mainline Station: Nuneaton (9 miles)
Nearest Bus Station: Nuneaton & Hinckley (9 miles)
Car Parking: Ample free parking available
Coach Parking: Can cater for coach parties
Souvenir Shop(s): Yes
Food & Drinks: Yes – Station Buffet

SPECIAL INFORMATION

Travel from the Grade II listed Shackerstone Station through the beautiful Leicestershire countryside with views of the adjoining Ashby Canal. Arrive at the award-winning Shenton Station and explore Bosworth Battlefield (1485) before making the return journey.

OPERATING INFORMATION

Operating Info: 2012 dates: Weekends and Bank Holidays from 3rd March to 28th October and Santa Specials on weekends from 1st December to Christmas Eve. Also open on Wednesday afternoons in July and August. Please check the web site for further details.
Opening Times: 10.55am to 5.10pm
Steam Working: From 11.15am to 4.00pm during high season and Sundays.
Prices: Adult Return £9.00
Child Return £5.00 (ages 5-15 years)
O.A.P. Return £7.00
Family Ticket £26.00
(2 adults and 2 children)

Detailed Directions by Car:
Follow the brown tourist signs from the A444 or A447 heading towards the market town of Market Bosworth. Continue towards the villages of Congerstone & Shackerstone and finally to Shackerstone Station. Access is only available via the Old Trackbed.

Beamish –
The Living Museum of the North

Address: Beamish – The Living Museum of the North, Co. Durham   DH9 0RG
Telephone Nº: (0191) 370-4000
Year Formed: 1970
Length of Line: ½ mile

Nº of Steam Locos: 9
Nº of Other Locos: 2
N.B.: Not all Locos are on display
Approx Nº of Visitors P.A.: 420,000
Web site: www.beamish.org.uk

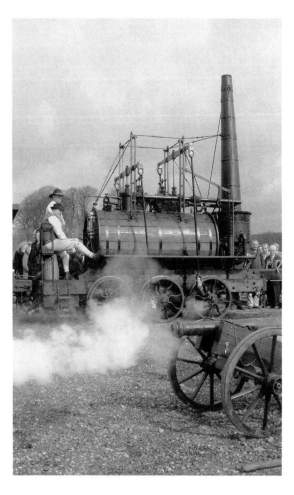

GENERAL INFORMATION

Nearest Mainline Station: Newcastle Central (8 miles); Durham City (12 miles)
Nearest Bus Station: Newcastle (8 miles); Durham (12 miles)
Car Parking: Free parking for 2,000 cars
Coach Parking: Free parking for 40 coaches
Souvenir Shop(s): Yes
Food & Drinks: Yes – self service tea room, licensed period Public House and a Coffee shop.

SPECIAL INFORMATION

A replica of William Hedley's famous 1813 locomotive "Puffing Billy" steams on the Pockerley Waggonway at Beamish alongside replicas of Locomotion and the Steam Elephant.

OPERATING INFORMATION

Opening Times: Open all year round: from 10.00am to 4.00pm in the Winter (November to March). Closed on Mondays and Fridays in the Winter. Open from 10.00am to 5.00pm during the Summer (April to October). Check for Christmas opening times.
N.B. Winter visits are centred on the Town and Tramway only. Other areas are closed and admission prices are reduced.
Allow 4-5 hours for a Summer visit and two hours in the Winter.
Steam Working: Daily during the Summer
Prices: Adult £17.50 in Summer
　　　　　Child £10.00 in Summer
　　　　　Senior Citizen £13.00 in Summer
Children under 5 are admitted free.
Special Family Tickets are available.

Detailed Directions by Car:
From North & South: Follow the A1(M) to Junction 63 (Chester-le-street) and then take A693 for 4 miles towards Stanley; From North-West: Take the A68 south to Castleside near Consett and follow the signs on the A692 and A693 via Stanley.

THE BLUEBELL RAILWAY

Address: The Bluebell Railway, Sheffield Park Station, near Uckfield   TN22 3QL
Telephone Nº: (01825) 720800
Year Formed: 1959
Location: Near Uckfield, East Sussex
Length of Line: 9 miles
Web site: www.bluebell-railway.com

Nº of Steam Locos: Over 30 with up to 3 in operation on any given day
Nº of Other Locos: –
Nº of Members: 10,000
Annual Membership Fee: £20.00 Adult
Approx Nº of Visitors P.A.: 175,000
Gauge: Standard

GENERAL INFORMATION

Nearest Mainline Station: Haywards Heath (approximately 8 miles)
Nearest Bus Station: Haywards Heath
Car Parking: Parking is available at Sheffield Park and Horsted Keynes Stations.
Coach Parking: Sheffield Park is best for coaches
Souvenir Shop(s): Yes
Food & Drinks: Yes – buffets and licensed bars & restaurant

SPECIAL INFORMATION

The Railway runs 'Golden Arrow' dining trains on Saturday evenings and Sunday lunchtimes. There is also a museum at Sheffield Park Station.

OPERATING INFORMATION

Opening Times: 2012 dates: Open every weekend throughout the year and also daily from 31st March to 2nd November inclusive. Also open during School holidays and for Santa Specials during December. Open from approximately 10.30am to 5.30pm
Steam Working: As above
Prices: Adult Return £13.50
            Child Return £6.80
            Family Return £37.00 (2 adult + 3 child)

Detailed Directions by Car:
Sheffield Park Station is situated on the A275 Wych Cross to Lewes road. Horsted Keynes Station is signposted from the B2028 Lingfield to Haywards Heath road.

BODMIN & WENFORD RAILWAY

Address: Bodmin General Station,
Losthwithiel Road, Bodmin, Cornwall
PL31 1AQ
Telephone Nº: (0845) 1259678
Year Formed: 1984
Location of Line: Bodmin Parkway to
Boscarne Junction, via Bodmin General
Length of Line: 6½ miles

Nº of Steam Locos: 11
Nº of Other Locos: 9
Nº of Members: 1,200
Annual Membership Fee: £14.00
Approx Nº of Visitors P.A.: 55,000
Gauge: Standard
Web: www.bodminandwenfordrailway.co.uk

GENERAL INFORMATION

Nearest Mainline Station: Bodmin Parkway (cross
platform interchange with the Bodmin & Wenford
Railway)
Car Parking: Free parking at Bodmin General
Coach Parking: Free parking at Bodmin General
Souvenir Shop(s): Yes
Food & Drinks: Yes

SPECIAL INFORMATION

The Railway has steep gradients and through tickets
to "Bodmin & Wenford Railway" are available from
all Mainline stations.

OPERATING INFORMATION

Opening Times: 2012 dates: Daily from 20th May
to 5th October. Also daily during Easter week and
other selected dates from February to May and
October plus Santa Specials on 2nd, 8th, 9th, 15th,
16th, 22nd, 23rd, 24th, 26th, 30th & 31st December
and 1st & 2nd January. Open 10.00am – 5.00pm on
most days.
Steam Working: Most trains are steam-hauled
except for most Saturdays when Diesels are used.
Daily steam throughout August.
Prices: Adult All Day Rover £11.50
 Child All Day Rover £6.00 (Under-3s free)
 Family Day Rover £30.00
 (2 adult + 2 child or 1 adult + 4 child)

Detailed Directions by Car:
From the A30/A38/A389 follow the signs to Bodmin Town Centre then follow the brown tourist signs showing
the steam engine logo to the Steam Railway on the B3268 Losthwithiel Road.

BO'NESS & KINNEIL RAILWAY

Address: Bo'ness Station, Union Street, Bo'ness, West Lothian   EH51 9AQ
Telephone Nº: (01506) 822298
Year Opened: 1981
Location of Line: Bo'ness to Manuel
Length of Line: 5 miles

Nº of Steam Locos: 26
Nº of Other Locos: 25
Nº of Members: 1,500
Annual Membership Fee: £22.00
Approx Nº of Visitors P.A.: 70,000
Gauge: Standard
Web site: www.srps.org.uk

GENERAL INFORMATION

Nearest Mainline Station: Linlithgow (3 miles)
Nearest Bus Station: Bo'ness (¼ mile)
Car Parking: Free parking at Bo'ness (and Birkhill) Stations
Coach Parking: Free parking at Bo'ness Station
Souvenir Shop(s): Yes
Food & Drinks: Yes

SPECIAL INFORMATION

In addition to the ten-mile journey, passengers should visit Scotland's largest railway museum at Bo'ness Station. The Railway and Museum are operated by volunteers from The Scottish Railway Preservation Society.

OPERATING INFORMATION

Opening Times: 2012 dates: Weekends from 31st March to 28th October. Also open for mid-week running on selected dates in April, June and October and on most days in July and August. Please contact the railway for further information. The museum is open daily from 31st March to 28th October.
Steam Working: On standard service days, 10.45am, 12.15pm and 2.05pm. The 3.35pm service may be diesel-hauled at weekends.
Prices: Adult Return £8.00   Child Return £4.00
Family Return £20.00   Concession Return £7.00
Note: Group discounts are also available.
Special fares may apply on Special Event Days.
Season Tickets for the Museum are £4.00

Detailed Directions by Car:
From Edinburgh: Take the M9 and exit at Junction 3. Then take the A904 to Bo'ness; From Glasgow: Take the M80 to M876 and then M9 (South). Exit at Junction 5 and take A904 to Bo'ness; From the North: Take M9 (South), exit at Junction 5, then take A904 to Bo'ness; From Fife: Leave the A90 after the Forth Bridge, then take A904 to Bo'ness.

BOWES RAILWAY

Address: Bowes Railway, Springwell Village, Gateshead, Tyne & Wear NE9 7QJ	**N° of Steam Locos**: 2
Telephone N°: (0191) 416-1847	**N° of Other Locos**: 5
Year Formed: 1976	**N° of Members**: Approximately 70
Location of Line: Springwell Village	**Annual Membership Fee**: £15.00
Length of Line: 1¼ miles	**Approx N° of Visitors P.A.**: 5,000
	Gauge: Standard
	Web site: www.bowesrailway.co.uk

GENERAL INFORMATION

Nearest Mainline Station: Newcastle Central (3 miles)
Nearest Bus Station: Gateshead Interchange (2 miles)
Car Parking: Free parking at site
Coach Parking: Free parking at site
Souvenir Shop(s): Yes
Food & Drinks: Yes

SPECIAL INFORMATION

Designed by George Stephenson and opened in 1826, the Railway is a scheduled Ancient Monument which operates unique preserved standard gauge rope-hauled inclines and steam hauled passenger trains.

OPERATING INFORMATION

Opening Times: The Springwell site is open for static viewing (no charges) on weekdays and some Saturdays throughout the year – 10.00am to 3.00pm.
Steam Working: As the 2012/2013 timetable had not been agreed when this book went to press, we suggest that readers check the railway's web site or contact the railway directly for further information.
Prices: No charges for visiting but admission fees are charged for special events. Please contact the railway or check the web site for further details.

Detailed Directions by Car:
From A1 (Northbound): Follow the A194(M) to the Tyne Tunnel and turn left at the sign for Springwell.
From A1 (Southbound): Take the turn off left for the B1288 to Springwell and Wrekenton.

BRESSINGHAM STEAM EXPERIENCE

Address: Bressingham Steam Museum, Bressingham, Diss, Norfolk IP22 2AB
Telephone Nº: (01379) 686900
Year Formed: Mid 1950's
Location of Line: Bressingham, Near Diss
Length of Line: 5 miles in total (3 lines)

Nº of Steam Locos: Many Steam locos
Nº of Members: 70 volunteers
Annual Membership Fee: –
Approx Nº of Visitors P.A.: 80,000+
Gauge: Standard, 2 foot, 10¼ inches and 15 inches
Web site: www.bressingham.co.uk

GENERAL INFORMATION

Nearest Mainline Station: Diss (2½ miles)
Nearest Bus Station: Bressingham (1¼ miles)
Car Parking: Free parking for 400 cars available
Coach Parking: Free parking for 30 coaches
Souvenir Shop(s): Yes
Food & Drinks: Yes

SPECIAL INFORMATION

In addition to Steam locomotives, Bressingham has a large selection of steam traction engines, fixed steam engines and also the National Dad's Army Museum, two extensive gardens and a water garden centre.

OPERATING INFORMATION

Opening Times: 2012 dates: Daily from 28th March to 4th November. Open from 10.30am to 5.00pm and until 5.30pm in June, July and August.
Steam Working: Almost every operating day except for most Mondays and Tuesdays in March, April, May, June, July, September and October. Please phone the Museum for further details.
Prices: Adult £10.50 (non-Steam) £12.95 (Steam)
Child £6.75 (non-Steam) £8.95 (Steam)
Family £27.50 (non-Steam) £35.00 (Steam)
Seniors £9.50 (non-Steam) £11.50 (Steam)

Detailed Directions by Car:
From All Parts: Take the A11 to Thetford and then follow the A1066 towards Diss for Bressingham. The Museum is signposted by the brown tourist signs.

BRISTOL HARBOUR RAILWAY

Address: Princes Wharf, City Docks, Bristol BS1 4RN **Telephone Nº:** (0117) 903-1570 **Year Formed:** 1978 **Location of Line:** South side of the Floating Harbour **Length of Line:** 1½ miles	**Nº of Steam Locos:** 2 **Nº of Other Locos:** 1 **Approx Nº of Visitors P.A.:** – **Gauge:** Standard **Web site:** mshed.org

GENERAL INFORMATION

Nearest Mainline Station: Bristol Temple Meads (1 mile)
Nearest Bus Station: City Centre (½ mile)
Car Parking: Pay & Display adjacent to M Shed
Coach Parking: Pay & Display adjacent
Souvenir Shop(s): In the M Shed Museum
Food & Drinks: Café in the Museum

SPECIAL INFORMATION

The brand new M Shed museum opened in 2011 on the site of the Industrial Museum. All the working exhibits have now resumed operations. Trains run alongside the harbour to link the M Shed with the SS Great Britain and Create Centre.

OPERATING INFORMATION

Opening Times: 2012 dates: 24th & 25th March; 7th, 8th, 9th, 21st & 22nd April; 5th, 6th, 7th, 19th & 20th May; 2nd to 5th, 23rd & 24th June; 14th, 15th, 29th & 29th July; 25th, 26th & 27th August; 8th, 9th, 22nd & 23rd September; 6th, 7th, 27th & 28th October; 3rd & 4th November. Trains run from 11.00am to 5.00pm.
Steam Working: Please contact the railway for further details.
Prices: All-day Rover £4.00
  M Shed to Create Return £3.00
  M Shed to Create Single £2.00
  M Shed to SS Great Britain Return £2.00
  M Shed to SS Great Britain Single £1.00
Note: Children under the age of 6 travel for free.

Detailed Directions by Car:
From All Parts: Follow signs to Bristol City Centre and then the Brown Tourist signs for the Museum. A good landmark to look out for are the 4 huge quayside cranes.

BUCKINGHAMSHIRE RAILWAY CENTRE

Address: Quainton Road Station, Quainton, Aylesbury, Bucks. HP22 4BY	**Nº of Steam Locos:** 30
Telephone Nº: (01296) 655720	**Nº of Other Locos:** 6
Year Formed: 1969	**Nº of Members:** 1,000
Location of Line: At Quainton on the old Metropolitan/Great Central Line	**Annual Membership Fee:** £25.00
	Approx Nº of Visitors P.A.: 35,000
	Gauge: Standard (also a Miniature line)
Length of Line: 2 × ½ mile demo tracks	**Recorded Info. Line:** (01296) 655450

GENERAL INFORMATION

Nearest Mainline Station: Aylesbury (6 miles)
Nearest Bus Station: Aylesbury
Car Parking: Free parking for 500 cars available
Coach Parking: Free parking for 10 coaches
Souvenir Shop(s): Yes
Food & Drinks: Yes

SPECIAL INFORMATION

In addition to a large collection of locomotives and carriages, the Centre has an extensive ½ mile outdoor miniature railway system operated by the Vale of Aylesbury Model Engineering Society.

Web site: www.bucksrailcentre.org
E-mail: office@bucksrailcentre.org

OPERATING INFORMATION

Opening Times: Daily for restricted viewing from Easter to October and for less restricted static viewing on Saturdays. Open 10.30am to 4.30pm.
Steam Working: Sundays and Bank Holidays from April to October and also on Wednesdays during the School holidays.
Prices: Adult £5.50, £10.00 and £12.00
Child £3.50, £7.00 and £9.00
(Under 5's travel free of charge)
Senior Citizen £4.50, £9.00 and £11.00
Family £15.00, £27.00 and £33.00
(2 adults + up to 4 children)
Note: Prices shown above are for restricted viewing, Steam Days and Special Event days respectively.

Detailed Directions by Car:
The Buckinghamshire Railway Centre is signposted off the A41 Aylesbury to Bicester Road at Waddesdon and off the A413 Buckingham to Aylesbury road at Whitchurch. Junctions 7, 8 and 9 of the M40 are all close by.

CALEDONIAN RAILWAY

Address: The Station, 2 Park Road, Brechin, Angus   DD9 7AF
Telephone Nº: (01561) 377760
Year Formed: 1979
Location of Line: From Brechin to the Bridge of Dun
Length of Line: 4 miles

Nº of Steam Locos: 5
Nº of Other Locos: 10
Nº of Members: 250
Annual Membership Fee: Adult £12.00; Family £15.00; OAP/Junior £5.00
Approx Nº of Visitors P.A.: 12,000
Gauge: Standard
Web site: www.caledonianrailway.com

GENERAL INFORMATION

Nearest Mainline Station: Montrose (4½ miles)
Nearest Bus Station: Brechin (200 yards)
Car Parking: Ample free parking at both Stations
Coach Parking: Free parking at both Stations
Souvenir Shop(s): Yes
Food & Drinks: Light refreshments are available

SPECIAL INFORMATION

Brechin Station is the only original Terminus station in preservation.

OPERATING INFORMATION

Opening Times: 2012 dates: Easter specials on 28th April; Christmas specials in December and every Sunday from 29th May to 2nd September. Also some Saturdays in July and August and for other Special Events throughout the year. Please contact the Railway for further details. Trains usually run from 10.30am to 5.05pm.
Steam Working: Steam service on every Sunday.
Prices: Adult Return £5.00
Child Return £3.00 (Under-3s ride free)
Senior Citizen Return £4.00
Family Return £16.00 (2 adult + 3 child)
Higher fares may apply for Special Event days.

Detailed Directions by Car:
From South: For Brechin Station, leave the A90 at the Brechin turn-off and go straight through the Town Centre. Pass the Northern Hotel, take the 2nd exit at the mini-roundabout then it is 150 yards to Park Road/St. Ninian Square; From North: For Brechin Station, leave the A90 at the Brechin turn-off and go straight through Trinity Village. Turn left at the mini-roundabout, it is then 250 yards to Park Road/St. Ninian Square. Bridge of Dun is situated half way between Brechin and Montrose. (Follow tourist signs).

CAMBRIAN HERITAGE RAILWAYS

Address: Old Station Building, Oswald Street, Oswestry SY11 4RE	**No of Steam Locos:** 3 (under repair)
Telephone No: (01691) 688763	**No of Other Locos:** 2 DMUs + others
Year Formed: 2009	**No of Members:** 500+
Location of Line: Llynclys and Oswestry	**Annual Membership Fee:** £15.00
Length of Line: Almost 1 mile at each site	**Approx No of Visitors P.A.:** 5,000
	Gauge: Standard
	Web site: www.cambrianrailways.com

GENERAL INFORMATION

Nearest Mainline Station: Gobowen (3 miles from Oswestry – 7 miles from Llynclys)
Nearest Bus Station: Oswestry
Car Parking: Limited parking at both sites
Coach Parking: Limited parking. Please contact the railway for further information.
Souvenir Shop(s): Yes
Food & Drinks: Available

SPECIAL INFORMATION

Cambrian Heritage Railways Ltd. lease 8½ miles of the former Cambrian Railways from Shropshire Council. The former Cambrian Railways Society and Trust are incorporated into CHR. The track is still in place from Gobowen to Llan y Blodwel. There are operations at Oswestry and Llynclys and a museum on site at Oswestry.

OPERATING INFORMATION

Opening Times: 2012 dates: Open every Saturday, Sunday and Bank Holiday from Easter to the 25th September. Also open on Sundays in October and December. Trains run from 11.00am to 4.00pm.
Steam Working: Please contact the Railway for information.
Prices: Adults £3.00
 Concessions £1.50
 Family £7.00
Note: All the above prices are for "Full Day Rover" tickets on Diesel-hauled days. Higher fares may apply on Steam-hauled days.

Detailed Directions by Car:
The Llynclys site is situated on the B4396 approximately 5 miles southwest of Oswestry, just off the A483 heading towards Welshpool. Turn left at Llyncly Crossroads towards Knockin. The entrance to the site is on the right after about 400 yards, immediately over the railway bridge. The Oswestry site is near the town centre and is clearly signposted.

CHASEWATER RAILWAY (THE COLLIERY LINE)

Address: Chasewater Country Park, Pool Road, Near Brownhills, Staffs, WS8 7NL **Telephone Nº**: (01543) 452623 **Year Re-formed**: 1985 **Location of Line**: Chasewater Country Park, Brownhills, near Walsall **Length of Line**: 2 miles	**Nº of Steam Locos**: 11 **Nº of Other Locos**: 13 **Nº of Members**: 800 **Annual Membership Fee**: Adult £15.00; Family £20.00; Concessions £10.00 **Approx Nº of Visitors P.A.**: 46,000 **Gauge**: Standard **Web site**: www.chaserail.com

GENERAL INFORMATION

Nearest Mainline Station: Walsall or Birmingham (both approximately 8 miles)
Nearest Bus Station: Walsall or Birmingham
Car Parking: Free parking in Chasewater Park
Coach Parking: Free parking in Chasewater Park
Souvenir Shop(s): Yes
Food & Drinks: Yes

SPECIAL INFORMATION

Chasewater Railway is based on the Cannock Chase & Wolverhampton Railway opened in 1856. The railway passed into the hands of the National Coal Board which then ceased using the line in 1965. Trains operate between Brownhills West and Chasetown.

OPERATING INFORMATION

Opening Times: 2012 dates: Sundays and Bank Holiday Mondays throughout the year plus Saturdays from 7th April to 27th October and Tuesdays and Thursdays from 26th July to 23rd August. Also Santa Specials in December. A regular service runs from 11.00am on operating days.
Steam Working: Please check the web site or phone for further details.
Prices: Adult Return £3.95
  Child Return £2.95 (Under-5s ride free)
  Family Return £9.95
All tickets offer unlimited rides on the day of issue.

Detailed Directions by Car:
Chasewater Country Park is situated in Brownhills off the A5 southbound near the junction of the A5 with the A452 Chester Road. Follow the Brown tourist signs on the A5 for the Country Park.

CHATHAM HISTORIC DOCKYARD RAILWAY

Address: Dock Road, Chatham	**Nº of Steam Locos**: 5
Telephone Nº: (01634) 823800	**Nº of Other Locos**: 3
Year Formed: 2001	**Nº of Members**: –
Location of Line: Chatham, Kent	**Approx Nº of Visitors P.A.**: Not known
Length of Line: ¾ mile	**Gauge**: Standard
	Web site: www.thedockyardrailway.co.uk

GENERAL INFORMATION

Nearest Mainline Station: Chatham (1½ miles)
Nearest Bus Station: Gillingham (1½ miles)
Car Parking: Available on site
Coach Parking: Available
Souvenir Shop(s): Yes
Food & Drinks: Available

SPECIAL INFORMATION

The Dockyard Railway is operated by North Kent Industrial Locomotive Society and runs demonstrations of freight steaming at Chatham's Historic Dockyard (www.chdt.org.uk).

OPERATING INFORMATION

Opening Times: Open one weekend per month. Please telephone or check the web site for details of special event dates.
Steam Working: Most operating days. Please note that the Railway does not offer train rides, merely demonstrations of engines in operation.
Prices: Adults £15.00
  Children (Aged 5-15 years old) £10.50
  Concessions £12.50
  Family Tickets £42.50
Note: Prices shown are for admission to the Dockyard and tickets are valid for 12 months. However, entrance to some special events is an additional charge.

Detailed Directions by Car:
From All Parts: Exit the M2 at Junction 3 and follow the A229 to Chatham. Follow the Brown tourist signs which clearly mark the correct route to the Dockyard.

CHINNOR & PRINCES RISBOROUGH RAILWAY

Address: Station Road, Chinnor, Oxon, OX39 4ER	**Nº of Steam Locos:** 1
Telephone Nº: (01844) 353535 (timetable)	**Nº of Other Locos:** 6
Year Formed: 1989	**Nº of Members:** 1,000
Location: The Icknield Line, Chinnor	**Annual Membership Fee:** Adult £15.00; Family £25.00; Child £5.00; OAP £10.00
Length of Line: 3½ miles	**Approx Nº of Visitors P.A.:** 15,000
Gauge: Standard	**Web Site:** www.chinnorrailway.co.uk

GENERAL INFORMATION

Nearest Mainline Station: Princes Risborough (4 miles)
Nearest Bus Station: High Wycombe (10 miles)
Car Parking: Free parking at site
Coach Parking: Prior arrangement preferred but not necessary
Souvenir Shop(s): Yes
Food & Drinks: Soft drinks and light snacks in Station Buffet. Buffet usually available on trains.

SPECIAL INFORMATION

The Chinnor & Princes Risborough Railway operates the remaining 3½ mile section of the former GWR Watlington Branch from Chinnor to Thame Junction.

OPERATING INFORMATION

Opening Times: 2012 dates: Sundays and Bank Holiday Mondays from 18th March to 28th October and also Santa Specials on weekends in December plus Mince Pie Specials from 29th to 31st December. Please check the railway's website for details of other bookable special and evening events during the year.
Steam Working: Operates from 10.15am to 4.15pm on Sundays and Bank Holidays
Prices: Adult Return £9.50   Child Return £5.00
Family Return £24.00 (2 adult + 2 child)
Senior Citizen Return £8.50

Detailed Directions by Car:
From All Parts: The railway at Chinnor is situated in Station Road just off the B4009. Junction 6 of the M40 is 4 miles away and Princes Risborough 4 miles further along the B4009. Once in Chinnor follow the brown Tourist signs to the railway.

CHOLSEY & WALLINGFORD RAILWAY

Address: Wallingford Station, 5 Hithercroft Road, Wallingford, Oxon, OX10 9GQ
Telephone Nº: (01491) 835067 (24hr info)
Year Formed: 1981
Location of Line: Wallingford, Oxon.
Length of Line: 2½ miles

Nº of Steam Locos: Visiting locos only
Nº of Other Locos: 4
Nº of Members: 250
Annual Membership Fee: £12.50
Approx Nº of Visitors P.A.: 9,700
Gauge: Standard
Web: www.cholsey-wallingford-railway.com

GENERAL INFORMATION

Nearest Mainline Station: Joint station at Cholsey
Nearest Bus Station: Wallingford (¼ mile)
Car Parking: Off road parking available
Coach Parking: Off road parking available
Souvenir Shop(s): Yes
Food & Drinks: Yes

SPECIAL INFORMATION

The Wallingford branch (now known as "The Bunk Line") was originally intended as a through line to Princes Risborough, via Watlington, but became the first standard gauge branch of Brunel's broad-gauge London to Bristol line.

OPERATING INFORMATION

Opening Times: Selected weekends from Easter until Christmas with trains running from 11.00am to 4.30pm – please phone the railway or check the web site for further details.
Steam Working: The railway will have visiting steam locomotives from time to time. Please contact the railway for further information.
Prices: Adult Return £8.00 (£6.00 diesel days)
Child Return £4.50 (£3.50 diesel days)
Concessionary Return £6.50 (£5.00 diesel)
Family Return £23.00 (£17.00 diesel days)
(2 adults + 2 children)
Prices: Prices may be subject to change for Engine visits and other special events.

Detailed Directions by Car:
From All Parts: Exit from the A34 at the Milton Interchange (between E. Ilsley and Abingdon). Follow signs to Didcot and Wallingford (A4130). Take Wallingford bypass, then turn left at the first roundabout (signposted Hithercroft Road). The Station is then ½ mile on the right.

CHURNET VALLEY RAILWAY

Address: Kingsley & Froghall Station, Froghall, Stoke-on-Trent ST10 2HA	City Railways, Cauldon Branch
Telephone Nº: (01538) 750755	**Nº of Steam Locos**: 6 (2 in operation)
Year Formed: 1978	**Nº of Other Locos**: 11 (3 in operation)
Location of Line: Kingsley & Froghall to Cheddleton	**Annual Membership Fee**: £14.00
	Approx Nº of Visitors P.A.: 70,000
Length of Line: 5¼ miles (plus a further 8 miles when operating over Moorland &	**Gauge**: Standard
	Web site: www.churnetvalleyrailway.co.uk

Photo courtesy of D.R. Gibson

GENERAL INFORMATION

Nearest Mainline Station: Stoke-on-Trent (12 miles)
Nearest Bus Station: Leek (5 miles)
Car Parking: Parking available on site
Coach Parking: Restricted space – please book in advance
Souvenir Shop(s): Yes
Food & Drinks: Yes

SPECIAL INFORMATION

Cheddleton Station is a Grade II listed building, Consall is a sleepy halt with Victorian charm, whereas Kingsley & Froghall has been rebuilt in NSR style and includes disabled facilities and a tearoom.

OPERATING INFORMATION

Opening Times: 2012 dates: Sundays from 29th January to 21st October, Weekends and Bank Holidays from 31st March to 30th September. Also open on Wednesdays in July and August. Santa Specials run on weekends and Wednesdays in December (pre-booking required). Trains run from 10.30am on most operating days or from 10.00am on Bank Holidays and Special Event days.
Steam Working: Most operating days except for Diesel Gala days.
Prices: Adult Day Rover £11.00
Child Day Rover £5.00 (Ages 4 to 14)
Senior Citizen Day Rover £9.00
Family Ticket Day Rover £28.00

Detailed Directions by Car:
From All Parts: Take the M6 to Stoke-on-Trent and follow roads to Ashbourne or Leek. Cheddleton Station is off the A520 Leek to Stone road (SatNav ST13 7EE). Kingsley & Froghall Station is off the A52 Ashbourne Road.

COLEFORD GWR MUSEUM

Address: The Old Railway Station, Railway Drive, Coleford GL16 8RH **Telephone Nº:** (01594) 833569 **Year Formed:** 1988 **Location of Line:** Coleford **Length of Line:** 100 yards	**Nº of Steam Locos:** 2 **Nº of Other Locos:** – **Approx Nº of Visitors P.A.:** Not known **Gauge:** 7¼ inches and Standard gauge **Web site:** www.colefordgwr.150m.com

GENERAL INFORMATION

Nearest Mainline Station: Lydney (7½ miles)
Nearest Bus Station: Gloucester (20 miles)
Car Parking: Available on site
Coach Parking: Available on site
Souvenir Shop(s): Yes
Food & Drinks: Tea and Coffee available only

SPECIAL INFORMATION

Based in the 1883 Goods Shed at Coleford, the Museum chronicles the history of railways in the Forest of Dean.

OPERATING INFORMATION

Opening Times: 2012 dates: Saturday afternoons and Bank Holidays throughout the year and Fridays from Easter until 4th November. Open from 2.30pm to 5.00pm and at other times by prior arrangement.
Steam Working: Easter Monday and other Bank Holidays. Please contact the Museum for details.
Prices: Adults £3.00 (admission to the museum)
Children £1.50 (admission to the museum)
Miniature Railway Rides £1.50
Peckett Footplate Visit £2.00 (if steaming)

Detailed Directions by Car:
From All Parts: From the M50 take the A40 at Ross-on-Wye to Monmouth then the A4136 towards Cinderford. Turn off the A4136 into Coleford and the Museum is located in the Town Centre.

COLNE VALLEY RAILWAY

Address: Castle Hedingham Station, Yeldham Road, Castle Hedingham, Essex, CO9 3DZ	**Nº of Steam Locos:** 4
	Nº of Other Locos: 11
	Nº of Members: 280
Telephone Nº: (01787) 461174	**Annual Membership Fee:** £11.00
Year Formed: 1974	**Approx Nº of Visitors P.A.:** 45,000
Location of Line: On A1017, 7 miles north-west of Braintree	**Gauge:** Standard
	Web Site: www.colnevalleyrailway.co.uk
Length of Line: Approximately 1 mile	

GENERAL INFORMATION

Nearest Mainline Station: Braintree (7 miles)
Nearest Bus Station: Hedingham bus from Braintree stops at the Railway (except on Sundays)
Car Parking: Parking at the site
Coach Parking: Free parking at site
Souvenir Shop(s): Yes
Food & Drinks: Yes – on operational days. Also Pullman Sunday Lunches – bookings necessary.

SPECIAL INFORMATION

The railway has been re-built on a section of the old Colne Valley & Halstead Railway, with all buildings, bridges, signal boxes, etc. re-located on site.

OPERATING INFORMATION

Opening Times: 2012 dates: Trains run every Sunday and Bank Holiday weekend from 18th March to 27th October. Open Wednesdays and Thursdays in August and School Holidays. Pre-booked parties any time by arrangement and various other special events. Please check the web site for further details.
Steam Working: Sundays 10.30pm to 4.00pm, Bank Holidays from 10.30am to 4.00pm and 10.30am to 3.30pm on midweek operating days.
Prices: Adult – Steam days £8.00; Diesel £6.00
Child – Steam £5.00; Diesel £4.00
Family (2 adults + 3 children) –
Steam £26.00; Diesel £20.00
Senior Citizen – Steam £7.00; Diesel £5.00

Detailed Directions by Car:
The Railway is situated on the A1017 between Halstead and Haverhill, 7 miles north-west of Braintree.

CREWE HERITAGE CENTRE

Address: Vernon Way, Crewe, CW1 2DB
Telephone Nº: (01270) 212130
Year Formed: 1987
Location of Line: Crewe Heritage Centre
Length of Line: 300 yards (Standard gauge) and 600 yards (7¼ inch gauge)

Nº of Steam Locos: 1
Nº of Other Locos: 2
Approx Nº of Visitors P.A.: 10,000
Gauge: 7¼ inches and Standard Gauge
Web site: www.creweheritagecentre.co.uk

GENERAL INFORMATION

Nearest Mainline Station: Crewe (¾ mile)
Nearest Bus Station: Crewe (½ mile)
Car Parking: Available on site
Coach Parking: None
Souvenir Shop(s): Yes
Food & Drinks: Tea and Coffee only

SPECIAL INFORMATION

Crewe Heritage Centre is an operational base for numerous mainline steam charters with various locomotives present throughout the year.

OPERATING INFORMATION

Opening Times: Weekends and Bank Holidays from Easter until the end of September. Open 10.00am to 4.30pm.
Steam Working: Please contact the Centre for details.
Prices: Adults £5.00
Children £2.00
Concessions £2.00
Family Tickets £10.00

Detailed Directions by Car:
From All Parts: Exit the M6 at Junction 16 and take the A500 into Crewe. Follow the brown tourist signs for "The Railway Age". The Heritage Centre is adjacent to Crewe Railway Station and next to the Tesco Supermarket.

THE DARTMOOR RAILWAY

Address: Okehampton Station, Station Road, Okehampton EX20 1EJ **Telephone Nº**: (01837) 55164 **Year Formed**: 1997 **Location of Line**: Meldon Quarry to Coleford Junction	**Length of Line**: 15½ miles **Nº of Steam Locos**: Visiting locos only **Nº of Other Locos**: 2 and DMUs **Gauge**: Standard **Web site**: www.dartmoor-railway.co.uk

GENERAL INFORMATION

Nearest Mainline Station: Crediton
Nearest Bus Station: Okehampton
Car Parking: Okehampton Station and some spaces at Sampford Courtenay Station – all free of charge
Coach Parking: Okehampton Station
Souvenir Shop(s): Yes
Food & Drinks: Okehampton Buffet is open from Friday to Sunday throughout the year. The Buffet is fully licensed.

SPECIAL INFORMATION

The railway operates on the route of the old Southern Railway line through the mid-Devon countryside to the northern slopes of Dartmoor National Park.

OPERATING INFORMATION

Opening Times: 2012 dates: Weekends and daily during the School Holidays from 6th April until the end of October. Please contact the railway for further details.
Steam Working: Visiting locomotives only. Please contact the railway for further information.
Prices: Vary depending upon the destination. Please contact the railway for further information.

Detailed Directions by Car:
From All Parts: Take the A30 Exeter to Launceston dual carriageway and exit at the Okehampton turn-off. Once in town, follow the brown tourist signs up the hill to Okehampton Station.

DARTMOUTH STEAM RAILWAY & RIVER BOAT COMPANY

Address: Queen's Park Station, Torbay Road, Paignton TQ4 6AF	**Nº of Steam Locos:** 6
Telephone Nº: (01803) 555872	**Nº of Other Locos:** 3
E-mail: carolyn@dsrrb.co.uk	**Nº of Members:** –
Year Formed: 1973	**Annual Membership Fee:** –
Location of Line: Paignton to Kingswear	**Approx Nº of Visitors P.A.:** 350,000
Length of Line: 7 miles	**Gauge:** Standard
	Web site: www.dartmouthrailriver.co.uk

GENERAL INFORMATION

Nearest Mainline Station: Paignton (adjacent)
Nearest Bus Station: Paignton (2 minutes walk)
Car Parking: Multi-storey or Mainline Station
Coach Parking: Multi-storey (3 minutes walk)
Souvenir Shop(s): Yes – at Paignton & Kingswear
Food & Drinks: Yes – at Paignton & Kingswear

SPECIAL INFORMATION

A passenger ferry is available from Kingswear Station across to Dartmouth. Combined excursions are also available including train and river trips.

OPERATING INFORMATION

Opening Times: Open daily from April to October (inclusive) and for Santa Specials during dates in December. Please contact the railway for further information.
Steam Working: Trains run throughout the day from 10.30am to 5.00pm.
Prices: Adult Return £13.00 (Includes ferry charge)
Child Return £8.50 (Includes ferry charge)
Family Return £34.99
2 adults and 2 children
(Includes ferry charge)
Note: Cheaper fares are charged for shorter journeys

Detailed Directions by Car:
From All Parts: Take the M5 to Exeter and then the A380 to Paignton.

DEAN FOREST RAILWAY

Address: Norchard Centre, Forest Road; Lydney, Gloucestershire GL15 4ET	**N° of Steam Locos**: 7 (4 working)
	N° of Other Locos: 18
Telephone N°: (01594) 845840	**N° of Members**: 1,000
Information Line: (01594) 843423 (24 hr.)	**Annual Membership Fee**: Adult £14.00;
Year Formed: 1970	Family (4 persons) £17.00
Location of Line: Lydney, Gloucestershire	**Approx N° of Visitors P.A.**: 35,000
Length of Line: 4½ miles	**Gauge**: Standard
	Web site: www.deanforestrailway.co.uk

GENERAL INFORMATION

Nearest Mainline Station: Lydney (200 metres)
Nearest Bus Station: Lydney Town (400 metres)
Car Parking: 600 spaces available at Norchard
Coach Parking: Ample space available
Souvenir Shop(s): Yes + a Museum
Food & Drinks: Yes – on operational days only

SPECIAL INFORMATION

Dean Forest Railway preserves the sole surviving line of the Severn and Wye Railway. The Railway has lengthened the line to a total of 4½ miles and Norchard to Parkend is now open for steam train operation giving a round trip of 9 miles.

OPERATING INFORMATION

Opening Times: 2012 dates: Norchard is open every day for viewing. Trains operate on Sundays from 4th March to 11th November, on most Wednesdays and Saturdays from 4th April to 24th October, Thursdays in August and various other dates. Phone or check the railway's web site for further details.
Steam Working: Most services are steam-hauled – check the web site or phone for details. Trains depart Norchard at various times from 10.35am to 3.30pm.
Prices: Adult Return £11.00   OAP Return £10.00
     Child Return £5.00 (Under-5s free)
     Family Ticket £30.00 (2 adults + 2 children)
Note: Fares may differ on Special Event days.

Detailed Directions by Car:
From M50 & Ross-on-Wye: Take the B4228 and B4234 via Coleford to reach Lydney. Norchard is located on the B4234, ¾ mile north of Lydney Town Centre; From Monmouth: Take the A4136 and B4431 onto the B4234 via Coleford; From South Wales: Take the M4 then M48 onto the A48 via Chepstow to Lydney; From Midlands/Gloucester: Take the M5 to Gloucester then the A48 to Lydney; From the West Country: Take the M4 and M48 via the 'Old' Severn Bridge to Chepstow and then the A48 to Lydney.

DERWENT VALLEY LIGHT RAILWAY

Address: Murton Park, Murton Lane, Murton, York YO19 5UF	**N° of Steam Locos**: 2
	N° of Other Locos: 5
Telephone N°: (01904) 489966	**N° of Members**: 80
Year Formed: 1991	**Annual Membership Fee**: £10.00
Location of Line: Murton, near York	**Approx N° of Visitors P.A.**: 15,000
Length of Line: ½ mile	**Gauge**: Standard
	Web site: www.dvlr.org.uk

GENERAL INFORMATION

Nearest Mainline Station: York (4 miles)
Nearest Bus Station: York (4 miles)
Car Parking: Large free car park at the site
Coach Parking: Free at the site
Souvenir Shop(s): Yes
Food & Drinks: Yes – as above

SPECIAL INFORMATION

The site is the remnants of the Derwent Valley Railway which was the last privately owned railway in England, originally opened in 1913.

OPERATING INFORMATION

Opening Times: 2012 dates: Sundays and Bank Holidays from 6th April until the end of September. Santa Specials also run during dates in December.
Steam Working: Second and last Sunday in the month and Bank Holidays – 10.30am to 4.15pm.
Prices: Adult £6.00
Child £4.00
Senior Citizens/Students £5.00
Family Tickets £16.00 (2 adult + 4 children)

Detailed Directions by Car:
From All Parts: The railway is well signposted for the Yorkshire Museum of Farming from the A64 (York to Scarborough road), the A1079 (York to Hull road) and the A166 (York to Bridlington road).

DIDCOT RAILWAY CENTRE

Address: Didcot Railway Centre, Didcot, Oxfordshire OX11 7NJ **Telephone Nº**: (01235) 817200 **Year Formed**: 1961 **Location of Line**: Didcot **Length of Line**: ¾ mile **Gauge**: Standard and 7 foot ¼ inch	**Nº of Steam Locos**: 23 **Nº of Other Locos**: 2 **Nº of Members**: 4,400 **Annual Membership Fee**: Full £26.00; Over 60/Under 18 £18.00; Family £33.00 **Approx Nº of Visitors P.A.**: 70,000 **Web Site**: www.didcotrailwaycentre.org.uk

GENERAL INFO

Nearest Mainline Station: Didcot Parkway (adjacent)
Nearest Bus Station: Buses to Didcot call at the Railway station
Car Parking: BR car park adjacent
Coach Parking: Further details on application
Souvenir Shop(s): Yes
Food & Drinks: Yes

SPECIAL INFO

The Centre is based on a Great Western Railway engine shed and is devoted to the re-creation of part of the GWR including Brunel's broad gauge railway and a newly built replica of the Fire Fly locomotive of 1840.

OPERATING INFO

Opening Times: 2012 dates: Weekends all year round, open daily during most school holidays and also from 2nd June to 16th September. Weekends and Steam days open 10.30am to 5.00pm. Other days and during Winter open 10.30am to 4.00pm.
Steam Working: Bank Holidays and most weekends until 27th August. Wednesdays from 25th July to 29th August. Phone or check the web site for details of Autumn steam days.
Prices: Adult £5.00–£10.00
Child £4.00–£10.00
Senior Citizen £4.50–£9.00
Discounted family tickets are often available (2 adults + 2 children). Prices vary depending on the events.

Detailed Directions by Car:
From East & West: Take the M4 to Junction 13 then the A34 and A4130 (follow brown Tourist signs to Didcot Railway Centre); From North: The Centre is signed from the A34 to A4130.

DOWNPATRICK & COUNTY DOWN RAILWAY

Address: Market Street, Downpatrick,
Co. Down, Northern Ireland
Telephone N°: (07790) 802049
Year Formed: 1985
Location of Line: Downpatrick
Length of Line: 2 miles
Gauge: Irish Standard (5 foot 3 inches)

N° of Steam Locos: 3
N° of Other Locos: 5
N° of Members: 200
Annual Membership Fee: Adult £25.00,
Family £50.00, Concessions £20.00
Approx N° of Visitors P.A.: 13,000
Web: www.downrail.co.uk

GENERAL INFORMATION

Nearest Mainline Station: –
Nearest Bus Station: Adjacent to Station
Car Parking: Ample parking adjacent to Station
Coach Parking: Ample parking adjacent to Station
Souvenir Shop(s): Yes
Food & Drinks: Yes

SPECIAL INFORMATION

This is the only operating Standard (5' 3") Gauge
Heritage Railway in Ireland.

OPERATING INFORMATION

Opening Times: The Museum is open daily from
June to September.
Steam Working: 2012 dates: 7th to 9th April and
weekends from 16th June to 9th September
(includes August Bank Holiday). Also Halloween
Ghost Trains on dates in October and Santa Specials
on some dates in December. Please contact the
railway for further details. Trains usually run from
2.00pm to 5.00pm.
Prices: Adult Return £5.50
             Child Return £4.50
             Concessionary Return £4.50

Detailed Directions by Car:
From Belfast take the A7 Downpatrick Road. Upon arrival in Downpatrick, follow the brown tourist signs and
the Railway Museum is adjacent to the bus station.

EAST ANGLIAN RAILWAY MUSEUM

Address: Chappel & Wakes Colne Station, Colchester, Essex CO6 2DS	**N° of Steam Locos:** 5 **Other Locos:** 4
Telephone N°: (01206) 242524	**N° of Members:** 750
Year Formed: 1969	**Annual Membership Fee:** Adult £20.00; Senior Citizen £15.00
Location of Line: 6 miles west of Colchester on Marks Tey to Sudbury branch	**Approx N° of Visitors P.A.:** 40,000
Length of Line: A third of a mile	**Gauge:** Standard
	Web site: www.earm.co.uk

GENERAL INFORMATION

Nearest Mainline Station: Chappel & Wakes Colne (adajcent)
Nearest Bus Stop: Wakes Colne Post Office (400 yards)
Car Parking: Free parking at site
Coach Parking: Free parking at site
Souvenir Shop(s): Yes
Food & Drinks: Snacks and drinks are available

SPECIAL INFORMATION

The museum has the most comprehensive collection of railway architecture & engineering in the region. The railway also has a miniature railway that usually operates on steam days.

OPERATING INFORMATION

Opening Times: Open daily 10.00am to 4.30pm. Steam days open from 11.00am to 4.30pm. Closed on Christmas Day and Boxing Day.
Steam Working: Steam days are held every month from April to August and also in October and December. Bank Holidays are also Steam days. Check the web site for further details.
Prices: Adult £4.50 static viewing; £8.00 Steam
   Child £2.00 static viewing; £4.00 Steam
   O.A.P. £4.00 static viewing; £7.00 Steam
   Family £10.00 static viewing; £20.00 Steam
Children under the age of 4 are admitted free of charge. A 10% discount is available for bookings for more than 10 people. A 10% discount is also available for visitors who visit using Mainline trains!

Detailed Directions by Car:
From North & South: Turn off the A12 south west of Colchester onto the A1124 (formerly the A604). The Museum is situated just off the A1124; From West: Turn off the A120 just before Marks Tey (signposted).

EAST KENT RAILWAY

Address: Station Road, Shepherdswell, Dover, Kent CT15 7PD **Telephone N°:** (01304) 832042 **Year Formed:** 1985 **Location of Line:** Between Shepherdswell and Eythorne **Length of Line:** 2 miles	**N° of Steam Locos:** None at present **N° of Other Locos:** 7 + 2 DMUs **N° of Members:** 250 **Annual Membership Fee:** £15.00 (Adult) **Approx N° of Visitors P.A.:** 4,500 **Gauge:** Standard gauge and also 5 inch miniature gauge **Web site:** www.eastkentrailway.co.uk

GENERAL INFORMATION

Nearest Mainline Station: Shepherdswell (50 yards)
Car Parking: Available Shepherdswell and Eythorne
Coach Parking: In adjacent Station Yard
Souvenir Shop(s): Yes
Food & Drinks: Yes

SPECIAL INFORMATION

The East Kent Railway was originally built between 1911 and 1917 to service Tilmanstone Colliery. Closed in the mid-1980's, the railway was re-opened in 1995.

OPERATING INFORMATION

Opening Times: The 2012 operating season begins with a 'Travel for a Pound' day on 25th March and then runs from 6th April until 16th September. Trains run every Sunday and Bank Holiday during this period plus Saturdays in August and during some special events including Halloween and Santa Specials. Contact the railway for further details.
Steam Working: None at present.
Prices: Adult £7.00   Child £4.00
           Senior Citizens £6.00
           Family £19.00 (2 Adults and 2 Children)

Detailed Directions by Car:
From the A2: Take the turning to Shepherdswell and continue to the village. Pass the shop on the left and cross the railway bridge. Take the next left (Station Road) signposted at the traffic lights for the EKR; From the A256: Take the turning for Eythorne at the roundabout on the section between Eastry and Whitfield. Follow the road through Eythorne. Further on you will cross the railway line and enter Shepherdswell. After a few hundred yards take the right turn signposted for the EKR.

EAST LANCASHIRE RAILWAY

Address: Bolton Street Station, Bury, Lancashire BL9 0EY
Telephone Nº: (0161) 764-7790
Year Formed: 1968
Location of Line: Heywood, Bury and Rawtenstall
Length of Line: 12 miles

Nº of Steam Locos: 14
Nº of Other Locos: 16
Nº of Members: 4,500
Annual Membership Fee: £19.00
Approx Nº of Visitors P.A.: 110,000
Gauge: Standard
Web site: www.east-lancs-rly.co.uk

GENERAL INFORMATION

Nearest Mainline Station: Manchester (then Metro Link to Bury)
Nearest Bus Station: ¼ mile
Car Parking: Adjacent
Coach Parking: Adjacent
Souvenir Shop(s): Yes
Food & Drinks: Yes

SPECIAL INFORMATION

Originally opened in 1846, the East Lancashire Railway was re-opened in 1987.

OPERATING INFORMATION

Opening Times: Every weekend & Bank Holiday 9.00am to 5.00pm. Also Wednesday to Friday from 4th April to 28th September. A number of special events also run throughout the year.
Steam Working: Most trains are steam-hauled. Saturdays alternate Steam & Diesel. 2 engines in steam on Sundays.
Prices: Adult Return £13.00
Child Return £8.40
Concessionary Return £11.00
Family Return £34.00
Cheaper fares are available for shorter journeys.

Detailed Directions by Car:
From All Parts: Exit the M66 at Junction 2 and take the A56 into Bury. Follow the brown tourist signs and turn right into Bolton Street at the junction with the A58. The station is about 150 yards on the right.

EAST SOMERSET RAILWAY

Address: Cranmore Railway Station, Shepton Mallet, Somerset BA4 4QP	**Nº of Steam Locos**: 6
Telephone Nº: (01749) 880417	**Nº of Other Locos**: 5
Year Formed: 1971	**Nº of Members**: 480
Location of Line: Cranmore, off A361 between Frome and Shepton Mallet	**Annual Season Ticket Fee**: Single £32.00 Family £96.00
Length of Line: 3 miles	**Approx Nº of Visitors P.A.**: 20,000
	Gauge: Standard

GENERAL INFORMATION

Nearest Mainline Station: Castle Cary (10 miles)
Nearest Bus Station: Shepton Mallet (3 miles)
Car Parking: Space for 100 cars available
Coach Parking: Yes
Souvenir Shop(s): Yes
Food & Drinks: Yes

SPECIAL INFORMATION

Footplate experience courses available – phone (01749) 880417 for further details.

Web site: www.eastsomersetrailway.com

OPERATING INFORMATION

Opening Times: Complex, Museum and Engine Sheds open daily from April to December and Tuesdays, Thursdays, Saturdays, January to March. Closed on Mondays and Wednesdays in November.
Steam Working: 2012 dates: Weekends and Bank Holidays from 6th April to 30th September, Wednesdays from 6th June to 26th September and Thursdays in August. Santa Specials run on some December weekends. Special events on other dates. Open 10.00am to 4.00pm (5.30pm in the Summer).
Prices: Adult Return £8.50   Child Return £6.50
Senior Citizen Return £7.50   Family Return £26.00

Detailed Directions by Car:
From the North: Take A367/A37 to Shepton Mallet then turn left onto A361 to Frome. Carry on to Shepton Mallet and 9 miles after Frome turn left at Cranmore; From the South: Take A36 to Frome bypass then A361 to Cranmore; From the West: Take A371 from Wells to Shepton Mallet, then A361 to Frome (then as above).

ECCLESBOURNE VALLEY RAILWAY

Address: Station Road, Coldwell Street, Wirksworth DE4 4FB **Telephone Nº:** (01629) 823076 **Year Formed:** 2000 **Location of Line:** Wirksworth to Duffield **Length of Line:** 8½ miles	**Nº of Steam Locos:** 1 **Nº of Other Locos:** 8 (including DMUs) **Nº of Members:** 700+ **Annual Membership Fee:** £15.00 **Approx Nº of Visitors P.A.:** 15,000 **Gauge:** Standard **Web site:** www.e-v-r.com

GENERAL INFORMATION

Nearest Mainline Station: Duffield (adjacent)
Nearest Bus Station: Derby (13 miles)
Car Parking: Available at the Station
Coach Parking: Available at Wirksworth Station
Souvenir Shop(s): Yes
Food & Drinks: Yes

SPECIAL INFORMATION

The line is has been restored section by section and the Railway opened all 8½ miles in April 2011.

OPERATING INFORMATION

Opening Times: 2012 dates: Wirksworth to Duffield and Ravenstor on weekends and Bank Holidays from 17th March to 28th October. Trains also run on Tuesdays from 5th June to 25th September. Services usually start at 9.55am, the last return train to Wirksworth is 4.20pm and last train for return to Duffield is 3.10pm with more trains laid on for special event days. Wirksworth Station is open for static viewing throughout the week.
Steam Working: Some weekends from 7th April to 30th September and on other special event days.
Prices: Adult Day Rover £3.50 to £10.00
Child Day Rover £2.00 to £5.00
Concessions Day Rover £3.00 to £9.00
Family Day Rover £10.00 to £18.00
Note: Prices vary depending on journey length.

Detailed Directions by Car:
From All Parts: Exit the M1 at Junction 26 and take the A610 Ambergate then the A6 to Whatstandwell. Turn left onto the B5035 to Wirksworth and the station is at the bottom of the hill as you enter the town.

ELSECAR HERITAGE RAILWAY

Address: Wath Road, Elsecar, Barnsley, S74 8HJ	**N° of Steam Locos:** 5
Telephone N°: (01226) 746746	**N° of Other Locos:** 2
Year Formed: 1997	**N° of Members:** Approximately 60
Location of Line: Elsecar, near Barnsley	**Annual Membership Fee:** £15.00
Length of Line: 1 mile	**Approx N° of Visitors P.A.:** 20,000
	Gauge: Standard
	Web site: www.elsecarrailway.co.uk

GENERAL INFORMATION

Nearest Mainline Station: Elsecar
Nearest Bus Station: Barnsley
Car Parking: Large free car park at the site
Coach Parking: At the site
Souvenir Shop(s): Yes
Food & Drinks: Yes

SPECIAL INFORMATION

The Railway is based at the Elsecar Heritage Centre which is an antiques and craft centre with a wide range of displays and special events.

OPERATING INFORMATION

Opening Times: The Heritage Centre is open daily from 10.00am to 5.00pm throughout the year (but closed between 25th December and 2nd January). Trains run on Sundays, Bank Holidays and during Special Events throughout the year plus Wednesdays in August. Hourly services from 12.00pm to 4.00pm.
Steam Working: Some services are diesel-hauled with regular steaming during the Summer months. Please phone for further details.
Prices: Adults £4.00   Children £2.50
Senior Citizens £3.00
Admission to the site is free of charge except for during Special Events.

Detailed Directions by Car:
From All Parts: Exit the M1 at Junction 36 and follow the brown 'Elsecar Heritage' signs taking the A6135 for approximately 2 miles. Turn left onto Broad Carr Road for just under a mile, then right onto Armroyd Lane and right again onto Fitzwilliam Street. Free visitor car parking is available on Wentworth Road off the junction of Fitzwilliam Street and Wath Road.

EMBSAY & BOLTON ABBEY STEAM RAILWAY

Address: Bolton Abbey Station, Bolton Abbey, Skipton, N. Yorkshire BD23 6AF	**Nº of Steam Locos**: 14
Telephone Nº: (01756) 710614	**Nº of Other Locos**: 12
Year Formed: 1968	**Nº of Members**: 700
Location of Line: 2 miles east of Skipton	**Annual Membership Fee**: £15.00
Length of Line: 4½ miles	**Approx Nº of Visitors P.A.**: 107,000
	Gauge: Standard

GENERAL INFORMATION

Nearest Mainline Station: Skipton (2 miles), Ilkley (3 miles)
Nearest Bus Station: Skipton (2 miles), Ilkley (3 mls)
Car Parking: Large car park at both Stations
Coach Parking: Large coach park at both Stations
Souvenir Shop(s): Yes
Food & Drinks: Yes – Cafe + Buffet cars

SPECIAL INFORMATION

The line extension to Bolton Abbey opened in 1998.

Web site: www.embsayboltonabbeyrailway.org.uk

OPERATING INFORMATION

Opening Times: Every Sunday throughout the year. Weekends from Easter to the end of October and daily in the summer season until early September. Tuesdays in April, May, June, July and September. Santa Specials run on December weekends.
Steam Working: Steam trains depart Embsay Station at 10.30am, 12.00pm, 1.30pm, 3.00pm and 4.30pm on most days during the Main Season. Contact the railway for further details.
Prices: Adult Return £8.00
Child Return £4.00
Family Ticket £22.00 (2 adult + 2 children)
Different fares may apply on special event days.

Detailed Directions by Car:
From All Parts: Embsay Station is off the A59 Skipton bypass by the Harrogate Road. Bolton Abbey Station is off the A59 at Bolton Abbey.

FOXFIELD STEAM RAILWAY

Address: Caverswall Road Station, Blythe Bridge, Stoke-on-Trent, Staffs. ST11 9EA	**N° of Steam Locos**: 22
Telephone N°: (01782) 396210	**N° of Other Locos**: 15
Year Formed: 1967	**N° of Members**: Over 300
Location of Line: Blythe Bridge	**Annual Membership Fee**: Adult £12.00; Junior £6.00; Family £20.00
Length of Line: 3½ miles	**Approx N° of Visitors P.A.**: 25,000
Gauge: Standard	**Web site**: www.foxfieldrailway.co.uk

GENERAL INFORMATION

Nearest Mainline Station: Blythe Bridge (¼ mile)
Nearest Bus Station: Hanley (5 miles)
Car Parking: Space for 300 cars available
Coach Parking: Space for 6 coaches available
Souvenir Shop(s): Yes
Food & Drinks: Yes – Buffet and Real Ale Bar

SPECIAL INFORMATION

The Railway is a former Colliery railway built in 1893 to take coal from Foxfield Colliery. It has the steepest Standard Gauge adhesion worked gradient in the UK and freight trains can be seen on these gradients during the annual Steam Gala in July.

OPERATING INFORMATION

Opening Times: 2012 dates: Sundays & Bank Holiday Mondays from 1st April to 31st October. Also Wednesdays in July and August and weekends in December. Open 11.00am to 5.00pm.
Steam Working: 11.30am, 1.00pm, 2.30pm and 4.00pm although Special Event days also run trains at earlier times.
Prices: Adult Tickets – £7.50
Child Tickets – £3.00 (3-16 years old)
Senior Citizen Tickets – £5.50
Fares may vary on special event days.

Detailed Directions by Car:
From South: Exit M6 at Junction 14 onto the A34 to Stone then the A520 to Meir and the A50 to Blythe Bridge; From North: Exit M6 at Junction 15 then the A500 to Stoke-on-Trent and the A50 to Blythe Bridge; From East: Take the A50 to Blythe Bridge. Once in Blythe Bridge, turn by the Mainline crossing.

GLOUCESTERSHIRE WARWICKSHIRE RAILWAY

Address: The Station, Toddington, Cheltenham, Gloucestershire GL54 5DT	**N° of Steam Locos:** 11
Telephone N°: (01242) 621405	**N° of Other Locos:** 17
Year Formed: 1981	**N° of Members:** 3,500
	Annual Membership Fee: £16.00 (Adult)
Location of Line: 5 miles south of	**Approx N° of Visitors P.A.:** 70,000
Broadway, Worcestershire, near the A46	**Gauge:** Standard and Narrow gauge
Length of Line: 12 miles	**Web site:** www.gwsr.com

GENERAL INFORMATION

Nearest Mainline Station: Cheltenham Spa or Ashchurch
Nearest Bus Station: Cheltenham
Car Parking: Parking available at Toddington, Winchcombe & Cheltenham Racecourse Stations
Coach Parking: Parking available as above
Souvenir Shop(s): Yes   **Food & Drinks:** Yes

SPECIAL INFORMATION

Due to a landslide, rebuilding work on the embankment to the north of Winchcombe means that two separate services are operating during 2012.

OPERATING INFORMATION

Opening Times: Weekends and Bank Holidays from April to December. Also during selected weekdays – please contact the railway for further details. Trains run from 10.30am to 5.00pm
Steam Working: On the Cheltenham Racecourse to Winchcombe section of the line only. Diesels are in use elsewhere on the line.
Prices: Adult Day Rover £14.00
Child Day Rover £6.00
Senior Citizen Day Rover £13.00
Family Ticket Day Rover £38.00
(2 Adults + 3 Children)
Under 5's travel free of charge apart from on some Special Event days.

Detailed Directions by Car:
Toddington is 11 miles north east of Cheltenham, 5 miles south of Broadway just off the B4632 (old A46). Exit the M5 at Junction 9 towards Stow-on-the-Wold for the B4632. The Railway is clearly visible from the B4632.

GREAT CENTRAL RAILWAY

Address: Great Central Station, Great Central Road, Loughborough, Leicestershire LE11 1RW
Telephone Nº: (01509) 632323
Year Formed: 1969
Location of Line: From Loughborough to Leicester

Length of Line: 8 miles
Nº of Steam Locos: 10
Nº of Other Locos: 11
Nº of Members: 5,000
Annual Membership Fee: £20.00
Approx Nº of Visitors P.A.: 100,000
Gauge: Standard

GENERAL INFORMATION

Nearest Mainline Station: Loughborough (1 mile)
Nearest Bus Station: Loughborough (½ mile)
Car Parking: Street parking outside the Station
Coach Parking: Car parks at Quorn & Woodhouse, Rothley and Leicester North
Souvenir Shop(s): Yes
Food & Drinks: Yes – Buffet or Restaurant cars are usually available for snacks or other meals

Web site: www.gcrailway.co.uk

SPECIAL INFORMATION

The aim of the GCR is to recreate the experience of British main line railway operation during the best years of steam locomotives.

OPERATING INFORMATION

Opening Times: 2012 dates: Weekends throughout the year, Wednesdays from July to September and Tuesday and Thursdays 19th July to 1st September. Santa Specials in December and other dates throughout the year. Contact the railway for details.
Steam Working: Weekends, Bank Holidays and some Special Events throughout the year.
Prices: Adult Day ticket £14.00
Child Day ticket £9.00
Senior Citizen Day ticket £12.00
Family Day Ticket £32 (2 adults + 3 children)

Detailed Directions by Car:
Great Central Road is on the South East side of Loughborough and is clearly signposted from the A6 Leicester Road and A60 Nottingham Road.

GREAT CENTRAL RAILWAY (NOTTINGHAM)

Address: Nottingham Transport Heritage Centre, Mere Way, Ruddington, Nottingham NG11 6NX **Telephone Nº:** (0115) 940-5705 **Fax Nº:** (0115) 940-5905 **Year Formed:** 1990 (Opened in 1994) **Location of Line:** Ruddington to Loughborough Junction	**Length of Line:** 9 miles **Nº of Steam Locos:** 6 **Nº of Other Locos:** 10 **Nº of Members:** 750 **Annual Membership Fee:** £14.00 **Approx Nº of Visitors P.A.:** 15,000 **Gauge:** Standard **Web site:** www.gcrn.co.uk

GENERAL INFO

Nearest Mainline Station: Nottingham (5 miles)
Nearest Bus Station: Bus service from Nottingham to Ruddington
Car Parking: Free parking at site
Coach Parking: Free parking at site
Souvenir Shop(s): Yes
Food & Drinks: Yes

SPECIAL INFORMATION

The Heritage Centre covers an area of more than eleven acres and is set within the Rushcliffe Country Park in Ruddington. Trains run to Loughborough Junction or Rushcliffe Halt.

OPERATING INFO

Opening Times: Sundays and Bank Holidays plus some Saturdays from Easter until October. Open 10.45am to 5.00pm. Also open for Santa Specials on December weekends.
Steam Working: Steam service runs from 11.30am
Prices: Adult £7.00 – £8.50
Child £3.50 – £4.00
Senior Citizens £6.00–£7.50
Family £16.00 – £20.00
(2 adults + 3 children)
Note: Prices vary depending on the journey length and unlimited day rover tickets are also available.

Detailed Directions by Car:
From All Parts: The centre is situated off the A60 Nottingham to Loughborough Road and is signposted just south of the traffic lights at Ruddington.

GWILI RAILWAY

Address: Bronwydd Arms Station, Bronwydd Arms, Carmarthen SA33 6HT **Telephone No:** (01267) 238213 **E-mail:** company@gwili-railway.co.uk **Year Formed:** 1975 **Location of Line:** Near Carmarthen, South Wales **Length of Line:** 2½ miles	**No of Steam Locos:** 5 **No of Other Locos:** 6 **No of Members:** 900 shareholders, 450 Society members **Annual Membership Fee:** £15.00 **Approx No of Visitors P.A.:** 24,000 **Gauge:** Standard **Web site:** www.gwili-railway.co.uk

GENERAL INFORMATION

Nearest Mainline Station: Carmarthen (3 miles)
Nearest Bus Station: Carmarthen (3 miles)
Car Parking: Free parking at Bronwydd Arms except for a few special occasions
Coach Parking: Free parking at Bronwydd Arms
Souvenir Shop(s): Yes
Food & Drinks: Yes

SPECIAL INFORMATION

Gwili Railway was the first Standard Gauge preserved railway in West Wales. There is a riverside picnic area and Miniature railway at Llwyfan Cerrig Station and there is a Signal Box Museum at the Bronwydd Arms.

OPERATING INFORMATION

Opening Times: Tuesday to Thursday from April to July and also in September. Daily from the end of July to the end of August. Wednesdays and Sundays in October and Santa Specials run on weekends in December. Please phone or check the website for further details & information about Special Events.
Steam Working: All advertised trains are steam hauled. Trains run from 10.30am to 4.00pm in high season and 10.30am to 2.50pm at other times.
Prices: Adult £8.00
        Child £2.00 (Under-2s ride free of charge)
        Family £15.00 (2 adults + up to 2 children)
        Senior Citizens £7.00
Note: Discounts are available for larger groups (10+).

Detailed Directions by Car:
The Railway is three miles North of Carmarthen – signposted off the A484 Carmarthen to Cardigan Road.

HEAD OF STEAM – DARLINGTON RAILWAY MUSEUM

Address: North Road Station, Darlington, Co. Durham DL3 6ST
Telephone N°: (01325) 460532
Year Formed: 1975
Location of Line: Adjacent to North Road Station
Length of Line: ¼ mile

N° of Steam Locos: 4
N° of Other Locos: None
N° of Members: 800 family memberships
Annual Membership Fee: £10.00 (adult) £15.00 (family);   £10.00 (senior)
Approx N° of Visitors P.A.: 33,500
Gauge: Standard
Web site: www.head-of-steam.co.uk

GENERAL INFORMATION

Nearest Mainline Station: North Road (adjacent)
Nearest Bus Station: Darlington (1 mile)
Car Parking: Free parking at site
Coach Parking: Free parking at site
Souvenir Shop(s): Yes
Food & Drinks: Cafe open 11.00am to 2.00pm (until 3.00pm at weekends).

SPECIAL INFORMATION

The museum is an 1842 station on the route of the Stockton and Darlington Railway and is devoted to the Railways of north-east England.

OPERATING INFORMATION

Opening Times: The Museum is open daily throughout the year but is closed every Monday. from April to September and every Monday and Tuesday from October to March. Also closed on Christmas Day, Boxing Day and New Year's Day. Open 10.30am to 3.30pm April to September and from 11.00am to 3.00pm from October to March.
Steam Working: At various Special events throughout the year – please phone for details.
Prices: Adult £4.95
　　　　Child £3.00 (ages 5 and under enter free)
　　　　Senior Citizen £3.75
　　　　Family Ticket £10.00
　　　　　　(2 adults and up to 4 children)

Detailed Directions by Car:
From Darlington Town Centre: Follow the A167 north for about ¾ mile then turn left immediately before the Railway bridge; From A1(M): Exit at Junction 59 then follow A167 towards Darlington and turn right after passing under the Railway bridge.

HELSTON RAILWAY

Address: Trevarno Manor, Crowntown, Helston, Cornwall TR13 0RU	**N° of Steam Locos:** None
Contact Telephone N°: 07901 977597	**N° of Other Locos:** 2 (plus 1 DMU)
E-mail: manager@helstonrailway.co.uk	**N° of Members:** Approximately 1,000
Year Formed: 2002	**Annual Membership Fee:** £10.00
Location: Trevarno Estate, Helston	**Approx N° of Visitors P.A.:** Not known
Length of Line: 1 mile	**Gauge:** Standard
	Web site: www.helstonrailway.co.uk

GENERAL INFORMATION

Nearest Mainline Station: Camborne (6 miles)
Nearest Bus Station: Camborne
Car Parking: At Trevano Gardens
Coach Parking: At Trevano Gardens
Souvenir Shop(s): Yes
Food & Drinks: Light refreshments are available

SPECIAL INFORMATION

The railway is operated by the Helston Railway Preservation Society which was formed in 2002. The long term aim is to re-open a three mile section of the old Helston branch line running through Trevano Gardens, between Nancegollan and Helston Water-Ma-Trout.

OPERATING INFORMATION

Opening Times: Every Sunday, Bank Holiday and Thursday from Easter until November. Open from 10.30am to 4.00pm.
Steam Working: Brake Van rides only at present but the railway hopes to have visiting steam locos on certain dates during 2012. Contact the railway for further information about these possible dates.
Prices: Adults £5.00 (Brake Van rides)
         Children £3.00 (Brake Van rides)
                 (Under-4s ride free of charge)
Note: Access to the railway is available via Trevarno Gardens car park. Trevarno Gardens is shutting after Easter 2012 so visitors will then be able to visit the railway without paying any additional fees.

Detailed Directions by Car:
The railway is situated within the Trevano Gardens estate which located is 1½ miles to the north of Helston, just off the B3303 between Crowntown and Nancegollan.

ISLE OF WIGHT STEAM RAILWAY

Address: The Railway Station, Havenstreet, Near Ryde, Isle of Wight PO33 4DS **Telephone Nº:** (01983) 882204 **Year Formed:** 1971 (re-opened) **Location:** Smallbrook Junction to Wootton **Length of Line:** 5 miles **Nº of Steam Locos:** 11	**Nº of Other Locos:** 3 **Nº of Members:** 1,450 **Annual Membership Fee:** £20.00 **Approx Nº of Visitors P.A.:** 110,000 **Gauge:** Standard **Talking Timetable:** (01983) 884343 **Web site:** www.iwsteamrailway.co.uk

GENERAL INFORMATION

Nearest Mainline Station: Smallbrook Junction (direct interchange)
Nearest Bus: From Ryde & Newport direct
Car Parking: Free parking at Havenstreet & Wootton Stations
Coach Parking: Free at Havenstreet Station
Souvenir Shop(s): Yes – at Havenstreet Station
Food & Drinks: Yes – at Havenstreet Station

SPECIAL INFORMATION

The IWSR uses mostly Victorian & Edwardian locomotives and carriages to recreate the atmosphere of an Isle of Wight branch line railway.

OPERATING INFORMATION

Opening Times: 2012 dates: Most days in April and May then daily from 27th May to 1st October (closed on 21st, 22nd & 28th September). Open on Wednesdays, Thursdays and Sundays in October and selected dates in November and December.
Please contact the railway for further information.
Steam Working: 10.30am to 4.00pm (depending on the Station)
Prices: Adult Return £9.50
Child Return £5.00 (Under-4s travel free)
Family Return £24.00
(2 adults + 2 children)
Note: First Class fares are higher than prices shown

Detailed Directions by Car:
To reach the Isle of Wight head for the Ferry ports at Lymington, Southampton or Portsmouth. From all parts of the Isle of Wight, head for Havenstreet (which is located 3 miles from Ryde and 3 miles from Newport), and follow the brown tourist signs.

KEIGHLEY & WORTH VALLEY RAILWAY

Address: The Station, Haworth, Keighley, West Yorkshire BD22 8NJ
Telephone Nº: (01535) 645214 (enquiries); (01535) 647777 (24 hour timetable)
Year Formed: 1962 (Line re-opened 1968)
Location of Line: From Keighley southwards through Haworth to Oxenhope
Length of Line: 4¾ miles

Nº of Steam Locos: 30
Nº of Other Locos: 10
Members: 4,500 (350 working members)
Annual Membership Fee: Adult £18.00; Adult life membership £360.00
Approx Nº of Visitors P.A.: 150,000
Gauge: Standard
Web Site: www.kwvr.co.uk

GENERAL INFORMATION

Nearest Mainline Station: Keighley (adjacent)
Nearest Bus Station: Keighley (5 minutes walk)
Car Parking: Parking at Keighley, Ingrow, Haworth (charged) and Oxenhope
Coach Parking: At Ingrow & Oxenhope (phone in advance)
Souvenir Shop(s): Yes – at Keighley, Oxenhope & Haworth (whose shop also sells books/DVDs)
Food & Drinks: Yes – at Keighley & Oxenhope when trains run.

OPERATING INFORMATION

Opening Times: 2012 dates: Weekends & Bank Holidays throughout the year. Daily from 2nd June to 9th September. Also open during Easter, Whit and February and October School holidays and from 26th to 31st December.
Steam Working: Early trains are Diesel; Steam runs from mid-morning on all operating days including the 4 weekends prior to Christmas when Santa Specials operate (pre-booking necessary for these).
Prices: Adult Return £10.00 (£14.00 Day Rover)
Child Return £5.00 (£7.50 Day Rover)
Family Day Rover £35.00
(2 adults + 3 children)

Detailed Directions by Car:
Exit the M62 at Junction 26 and take the M606 to its' end. Follow the ring-road signs around Bradford to Shipley. Take the A650 through Bingley to Keighley and follow the brown tourist signs to the railway. Alternatively, take the A6033 from Hebden Bridge to Oxenhope and follow the brown signs to Oxenhope or Haworth Stations.

THE KEITH & DUFFTOWN RAILWAY

Address: Dufftown Station, Dufftown, Banffshire, AB55 4BA **Telephone Nº:** (01340) 821181 **Year Formed:** 2000 **Location of Line:** Keith to Dufftown **Length of Line:** 11 miles	**Nº of Steam Locos:** None at present **Nº of Other Locos:** 2 **Nº of Members:** Approximately 400 **Annual Membership Fee:** Adult £11.00 **Approx Nº of Visitors P.A.:** Not known **Gauge:** Standard **Web:** www.keith-dufftown-railway.co.uk

GENERAL INFORMATION

Nearest Mainline Station: Keith (½ mile)
Nearest Bus Station: Elgin (Bus routes travel to both Keith and Dufftown)
Car Parking: Available at both Stations
Coach Parking: Available at both Stations
Souvenir Shop(s): Yes – at Keith Town Station
Food & Drinks: Available at Dufftown Station

SPECIAL INFORMATION

The Keith and Dufftown Railway is an eleven mile line linking the World's Malt Whisky Capital, Dufftown, to the market town of Keith. The line, which was reopened by volunteers during 2000 and 2001, passes through some of Scotland's most picturesque scenery, with forest and farmland, lochs and glens, castles and distilleries.

OPERATING INFORMATION

Opening Times: Weekends from Easter until the end of September and also on Fridays in June, July and August. Trains depart Dufftown from 11.25am until 4.40pm.
Steam Working: None at present
Prices: Adult Return £10.00
Child Return £5.00
Senior Citizen Return £8.00
Family Return £24.00
Note: Shorter journeys are cheaper.

Detailed Directions by Car:
Keith Town Station is located in Keith, on the A96 Aberdeen to Inverness Road; Dufftown Station is about 1 mile to the north of the Dufftown Town Centre just off the A941 road to Elgin.

KENT & EAST SUSSEX RAILWAY

Address: Tenterden Town Station, Tenterden, Kent   TN30 6HE
Telephone Nº: (01580) 765155
Year Formed: 1974
Location of Line: Tenterden, Kent to Bodiam, East Sussex
Length of Line: 10½ miles

Nº of Steam Locos: 12
Nº of Other Locos: 6
Nº of Members: 2,100
Annual Membership Fee: £23.00
Approx Nº of Visitors P.A.: 99,000
Gauge: Standard
Web site: www.kesr.org.uk

GENERAL INFORMATION

Nearest Mainline Station: Headcorn (8 miles)
Nearest Bus Station: Tenterden
Car Parking: Free parking available at Tenterden Town and Northiam Stations
Coach Parking: Tenterden & Northiam
Souvenir Shop(s): Yes
Food & Drinks: Yes

SPECIAL INFORMATION

Built as Britain's first light railway, the K&ESR opened in 1900 and was epitomised by sharp curved and steep gradients and to this day retains a charm and atmosphere all of its own.

OPERATING INFORMATION

Opening Times: From February to October and in December. The return journey time is 1 hour 55 minutes. Please phone the 24 hour talking-timetable for precise operating information: (01580) 762943
Steam Working: Every operational day
Prices: Adult Ticket – £15.00
Child Ticket – £10.00
Senior Citizen Ticket – £14.00
Family Ticket – £42.00
(2 adults + 3 children or 1 adult + 4 children)
Note: The prices shown above are for Day Rover tickets which allow unlimited travel on the day of purchase.

Detailed Directions by Car:
From London and Kent Coast: Travel to Ashford (M20) then take the A28 to Tenterden; From Sussex Coast: Take A28 from Hastings to Northiam.

LAKESIDE & HAVERTHWAITE RAILWAY

Address: Haverthwaite Station, near Ulverston, Cumbria LA12 8AL	**Nº of Steam Locos:** 8
Telephone Nº: (015395) 31594	**Nº of Other Locos:** 6
E-mail: info@lakesiderailway.co.uk	**Nº of Members:** 250
Year Formed: 1973	**Annual Membership Fee:** £12.00 Adult, £6.00 Juniors
Location of Line: Haverthwaite to Lakeside	**Approx Nº of Visitors P.A.:** 170,000
Length of Line: 3½ miles	**Gauge:** Standard
	Web site: www.lakesiderailway.co.uk

GENERAL INFORMATION

Nearest Mainline Station: Ulverston (7 miles)
Nearest Bus Station: Haverthwaite (100 yards)
Car Parking: Plenty of spaces – Charges from £1.00
Coach Parking: Free parking at site
Souvenir Shop(s): Yes
Food & Drinks: Yes

SPECIAL INFORMATION

Tickets which include train ride followed by a cruise on Lake Windermere or a visit to the Aquarium of the Lakes are also available from the Railway.

OPERATING INFORMATION

Opening Times: 2012 dates: Daily from 31st March to 4th November inclusive. Also open for Diesel weekends on 17th, 18th, 24th & 25th November. Santa Specials run on 1st, 2nd, 8th, 9th, 15th & 16th December. Also Thomas the Tank Engine weekends on 24th & 25th March and 10th and 11th November.
Steam Working: Daily from morning to late afternoon.

Prices: Adult Return £6.30   Single £3.80
  Child Return £3.20   Single £2.50
  Family Ticket £16.90

Note: Prices vary for Special Events and individual fares apply for combined tickets including other attractions.

Detailed Directions by Car:
From All Parts: Exit the M6 at Junction 36 and follow the brown tourist signs.

THE LAVENDER LINE

Address: Isfield Station, Isfield, near Uckfield, East Sussex TN22 5XB
Telephone Nº: (01825) 750515
Year Formed: 1992
Location of Line: East Sussex between Lewes and Uckfield
Length of Line: 1 mile

Nº of Steam Locos: 1
Nº of Other Locos: 3 + DEMU
Nº of Members: Approximately 400
Annual Membership Fee: £15.00
Approx Nº of Visitors P.A.: 12,500
Gauge: Standard
Web site: www.lavender-line.co.uk

GENERAL INFORMATION

Nearest Mainline Station: Uckfield (3 miles)
Nearest Bus Station: Uckfield (3 miles)
Car Parking: Free parking at site
Coach Parking: Can cater for coach parties – please contact the Railway.
Souvenir Shop: Yes
Food & Drinks: Yes – Cinders Buffet

SPECIAL INFORMATION

Isfield Station has been restored as a Southern Railway country station complete with the original L.B.S.C.R. signalbox.

OPERATING INFORMATION

Opening Times: Sundays throughout the year plus Wednesdays and Thursdays in August. Also open on Bank Holidays, daily during February and October School half-term holidays and for Santa Specials in December.
Steam Working: Please phone for details.
Prices: Adult £9.00
　　　　　Child £6.00
　　　　　Senior Citizen £7.00
　　　　　Family Ticket £28.00
　　　　　(2 adults + 3 children)
All tickets offer unlimited rides on the day of issue and prices may vary on special event days.

Detailed Directions by Car::
From All Parts: Isfield is just off the A26 midway between Lewes and Uckfield.

LINCOLNSHIRE WOLDS RAILWAY

Address: The Railway Station, Ludborough, Lincolnshire DN36 5SQ **Telephone N°:** (01507) 363881 **Year Formed:** 1979 **Location of Line:** Ludborough – off the A16(T) between Grimsby and Louth **Length of Line:** 1½ miles	**N° of Steam Locos:** 3 **Other Locos:** 7 **N° of Members:** 400+ **Annual Membership Fee:** £26.00 Family, £13.00 Adult, £8.00 Senior Citizen **Approx N° of Visitors P.A.:** 9,000 **Gauge:** Standard **Web:** www.lincolnshirewoldsrailway.co.uk

Photo courtesy of B. Wakefield

GENERAL INFORMATION

Nearest Mainline Station: Grimsby (8 miles)
Nearest Bus Stop: Ludborough (½ mile)
Car Parking: Available at Ludborough Station only
Coach Parking: Space for 1 coach only
Souvenir Shop(s): Yes
Food & Drinks: Yes

SPECIAL INFORMATION

The buildings and facilities at Ludborough have been completed and short steam trips commenced in 1998. A line extension to North Thoresby (1½ miles) is now open.

E-mail: contact@lincolnshirewoldsrailway.co.uk

OPERATING INFORMATION

Opening Times: 2012 dates: 18th & 25th March; 7th to 9th, 15th & 29th April; 6th, 7th & 20th May; 3rd to 5th & 17th June; 1st, 8th & 22nd July; 1st, 5th, 8th, 12th, 15th, 19th, 22nd, 26th, 27th & 29th August; 8th, 9th & 30th September; 14th, 24th & 28th October; 3rd & 25th November; 8th, 9th, 15th & 16th December for Santa Specials. Please note that advance bookings are essential for Santa Specials.
Steam Working: All operating days if possible.
Prices: Adults £7.00   Children £4.00
Senior Citizens £5.00
Family £18.00 (2 adults + 4 children)
Different fares may apply at Special Events.
Prices include unlimited rides throughout the day.

Detailed Directions by Car:
The Railway is situated near Ludborough, ½ mile off the A16(T) Louth to Grimsby road. Follow the brown tourist signs for ½ mile to Fulstow to reach the station. Do not turn into Ludborough but stay on the bypass.

LLANGOLLEN RAILWAY

Address: The Station, Abbey Road, Llangollen, Denbighshire LL20 8SN **Telephone Nº:** (01978) 860979 **Year Formed:** 1975 **Location of Line:** Valley of the River Dee from Llangollen to Carrog **Length of Line:** 7½ miles	**Nº of Steam Locos:** 14 **Other Locos:** 13 **Nº of Members:** 1,400 **Annual Membership Fee:** Adult £18.00; Family £25.00; Junior (under-16) £10.00 **Approx Nº of Visitors P.A.:** 110,000 **Gauge:** Standard **Web Site:** www.llangollen-railway.co.uk

Photograph courtesy of David Wilcock

GENERAL INFORMATION

Nearest Mainline Station: Ruabon (6 miles)
Nearest Bus Station: Wrexham (12 miles)
Car Parking: Llangollen Royal International Pavilion (SatNav post code: LL20 8SW)
Coach Parking: Market Street car park in town centre (SatNav post code: LL20 8PS)
Souvenir Shop(s): Yes – at Llangollen Station
Food & Drinks: Yes – at Llangollen, Berwyn, Glyndyfrdwy and Carrog Stations.

SPECIAL INFORMATION

The route originally formed part of the line from Ruabon to Barmouth Junction, closed in 1964. The railway has been rebuilt by volunteers since 1975, reopening to Carrog in 1996 and the aim is to open an extra 2½ miles to Corwen by Autumn 2012.

OPERATING INFORMATION

Opening Times: 2012 dates: Services run daily from 1st April to 7th October. Also on weekends in December and for Santa Specials near Christmas.
Steam Working: Phone the Talking timetable number for further details: (01978) 860951
Prices: Adult Day Rover £12.00
Child Day Rover £6.00
Family Day Rover £30.00 (2 adult + 2 child)
Senior Citizen Day Rover £10.00
Note: Tickets for shorter journeys are available.

Detailed Directions by Car:
From South & West: Go via the A5 to Llangollen. At the traffic lights turn into Castle Street to the River bridge; From North & East: Take the A483 to A539 junction and then via Trefor to Llangollen River bridge. The Station is adjacent to the River Dee.

LOCOMOTION – THE NATIONAL RAILWAY MUSEUM AT SHILDON

Address: Locomotion, Shildon,
County Durham   DL14 1PQ
Telephone Nº: (01388) 777999
Fax Nº: (01388) 771448
Year Formed: 2004
Location: Shildon, County Durham

Length of Line: Over ½ mile
Nº of Steam Locos: 60 locomotives and
other rail vehicles
Approx Nº of Visitors P.A.: 60,000+
Gauge: Standard
Web site: www.nrm.org.uk/locomotion

GENERAL INFORMATION

Nearest Mainline Station: Shildon (adjacent)
Nearest Bus Station: Durham
Car Parking: Available on site
Coach Parking: Available on site
Souvenir Shop(s): Yes
Food & Drinks: Yes

SPECIAL INFORMATION

This extensive site is the first regional branch of the
National Railway Museum and houses vehicles from
the National Collection in a purpose-built 6,000
square-foot building.

OPERATING INFORMATION

Opening Times: 2012 dates: Daily from 1st April to
3rd October – 10.00am to 5.00pm. The Collection
Building is open on Mondays and Tuesdays between
4th October 2012 to 31st March 2013 – 10.00am to
4.00pm. The rest of the site is open from Wednesday
to Sunday during the Winter season – also from
10.00am to 4.00pm although the Museum is closed
over the Christmas and New Year Holiday period.
Steam Working: During the Summer School
Holidays and on special event days – please phone to
confirm details.
Prices: Admission to the Museum is free of charge.
Train Rides: Adults £2.00   Concessions £1.00

Detailed Directions by Car:
From All Parts: Exit the A1(M) at Junction 58 and take the A68 and the A6072 to Shildon. Follow the Brown
tourist signs to Locomotion which is situated ¼ mile to the south-east of the Town Centre.

MANGAPPS RAILWAY MUSEUM

Address: Southminster Road, Burnham-on-Crouch, Essex CM0 8QG	**No of Steam Locos**: 6
Telephone No: (01621) 784898	**No of Other Locos**: 12
Year Formed: 1989	**Approx No of Visitors P.A.**: 20,000
Location of Line: Mangapps Farm	**Gauge**: Standard
Length of Line: ¾ mile	**Web site**: www.mangapps.co.uk
	E-mail: mangapps@tiscali.co.uk

GENERAL INFORMATION

Nearest Mainline Station: Burnham-on-Crouch (1 mile)
Nearest Bus Station: –
Car Parking: Ample free parking at site
Coach Parking: Ample free parking at site
Souvenir Shop(s): Yes
Food & Drinks: Yes – drinks and snacks only

SPECIAL INFORMATION

The Railway endeavours to recreate the atmosphere of an East Anglian light railway. It also includes an extensive museum with an emphasis on East Anglian items and signalling.

OPERATING INFORMATION

Opening Times: Closed during January and November, then open every weekend and Bank Holiday (except over Christmas) and daily during August. Santa Specials run during weekends in December. Please contact the railway for details of opening times during the School Holidays and Olympic Games or for any other information.
Steam Working: Bank Holiday Sundays and Mondays plus certain other dates. Diesel at other times. Please contact the railway for further details.
Prices: Adult – Steam £8.00; Diesel £7.00
Child – Steam £3.50; Diesel £3.00
Senior Citizen – Steam £7.00; Diesel £6.00
Note: Prices for special events may differ.

Detailed Directions by Car:
From South & West: From M25 take either the A12 or A127 and then the A130 to Rettendon Turnpike and then follow signs to Burnham; From North: From A12 take A414 to Oak Corner then follow signs to Burnham.

THE MIDDLETON RAILWAY

Address: The Station, Moor Road, Hunslet, Leeds LS10 2JQ
Telephone N°: (0113) 271-0320
Year Formed: 1960
Location of Line: Moor Road to Middleton Park
Length of Line: 1½ miles

N° of Steam Locos: 20
N° of Other Locos: 13
Annual Membership Fee: Adults £17.00
Approx N° of Visitors P.A.: 20,000
Gauge: Standard
Web Site: www.middletonrailway.org.uk

GENERAL INFORMATION

Nearest Mainline Station:
Leeds City (1 mile)
Nearest Bus Station: Leeds (1½ miles)
Car Parking: Free parking at site
Coach Parking: Free parking at site
Souvenir Shop(s): Yes
Food & Drinks: Yes

SPECIAL INFORMATION

The Middleton Railway is the oldest working railway in the world and was established in 1758 by Act of Parliament. The railway is also the first Standard Gauge line to be operated by volunteers and the first revenue-earning steam locomotive ran here in 1812. The railway also hosts a working museum housing a collection of Leeds built locomotives.

OPERATING INFORMATION

Opening Times: 2012 dates: Weekends and Bank Holidays from 31st March to the end of November plus Santa Specials in December. Also open on Wednesdays in August. Diesel services run at 40 minute intervals from 1.00pm to 4.20pm.
Steam Working: Every Sunday and Bank Holiday Monday from Easter to the end of November plus Santa Specials in December. Steam services run at 40 minute intervals from 11.00am to 4.20pm.
Prices: Adult £4.50   Child £2.50
            Family £12.00
                 (2 adults + 3 children)
Tickets provide for unlimited travel on the day of issue. For a full timetable and details of special events, please check the railway's web site or phone 0845 680-1758.
Note: Different prices may apply on Special Event days.

Detailed Directions by Car:
From the South: Take the M621 Northbound and exit at Junction 5. Turn right at the top of the slip road and take the 3rd exit at the roundabout. The Railway is 50 yards on the right; From the West: Take the M621 Southbound and exit at Junction 6. Turn left at the end of the slip road then left again into Moor Road at the next set of traffic lights. Bear right at the mini roundabout and the railway is on the left after 150 yards.

MID-HANTS RAILWAY (WATERCRESS LINE)

Address: The Railway Station, Alresford, Hampshire SO24 9JG **Telephone Nº:** (01962) 733810 General enquiries; (01962) 734866 Timetable **Year Formed:** 1977 **Location of Line:** Alresford to Alton **Length of Line:** 10 miles	**Nº of Steam Locos:** 24 (9 in steam) **Nº of Other Locos:** 8 **Nº of Members:** 3,500 **Annual Membership Fee:** Adult £25.00 **Approx Nº of Visitors P.A.:** 150,000 **Gauge:** Standard **Web Site:** www.watercressline.co.uk

Photo courtesy of Matt Allen

GENERAL INFORMATION

Nearest Mainline Station: Alton (adjacent) or Winchester (7 miles)
Nearest Bus Station: Winchester or Alton
Car Parking: Pay and display at Alton and Alresford Stations (Alresford free on Sundays & Bank Holidays)
Coach Parking: By arrangement at Alresford Station
Souvenir Shop(s): At Alresford, Ropley & Alton
Food & Drinks: Yes – Buffet on most trains. 'West Country' buffet at Alresford

SPECIAL INFORMATION

The railway runs through four fully restored stations and has a Loco yard and picnic area at Ropley.

OPERATING INFORMATION

Opening Times: 2012 dates: Weekends and Bank Holidays from January to October plus Tuesday to Thursday from May to the 20th September. Daily during the School holidays. Santa Specials run at weekends and on other dates in December.
Steam Working: All operating days although a Steam/DMU combination is sometimes in service.
Prices: Adult £14.00
Child (ages 2 to 16) £7.00 (Under-2s free)
Family £35.00 (2 adults + 2 children)
Prices shown above are for Day Rover fares.
A discount is available for pre-booked parties of 15 or more people. Write or call for a booking form.

Detailed Directions by Car:
From the East: Take the M25 then A3 and A31 to Alton; From the West: Exit the M3 at Junction 9 and take the A31 to Alresford Station.

MID-NORFOLK RAILWAY

Address: The Railway Station, Station Road, Dereham   NR19 1DF
Telephone Nº: (01362) 690633 or 851723
Year Formed: 1995
Location: East Dereham to Wymondham
Length of Line: 11 miles

Nº of Steam Locos: Visiting locos only
Nº of Other Locos: 8
Nº of Members: 1,000
Annual Membership Fee: £16.00
Approx Nº of Visitors P.A.: 16,000
Gauge: Standard
Web site: www.mnr.org.uk

GENERAL INFORMATION

Nearest Mainline Station: Wymondham (1 mile)
Nearest Bus Station: Wymondham or East Dereham – each ½ mile away
Car Parking: Available at Dereham Station
Coach Parking: Available at Dereham Station
Souvenir Shop(s): Yes – at Dereham Station
Food & Drinks: Yes – at Dereham Station

SPECIAL INFORMATION

The Mid-Norfolk Railway aims to preserve the former Great Eastern Railway from Wymondham to County School. The section from Wymondham to Dereham was opened to passenger and freight traffic in May 1999 and clearance work is now complete on the East Dereham to County School section.

OPERATING INFORMATION

Opening Times: 2012 dates: Weekends and Bank Holidays from 31st March to 4th November. Also on Wednesdays from 2nd May to 31st October and Thursdays from 7th June to 27th September. Santa Specials run on some dates in December.
Steam Working: Weekends and Bank Holidays from 30th July to 19th August inclusive with a visiting Steam locomotive.
Prices: Adult Return £7.00 (Diesel)
Child Return £3.50 (Diesel)
Senior Citizen Return £6.00 (Diesel)
Adult Return £10.00 (Steam days)
Child Return £5.00 (Steam days)
Senior Citizen Return £9.00 (Steam days)

Detailed Directions by Car:
From All Parts: From the A47 bypass, turn into Dereham and follow the signs for the Town Centre. Turn right at the BP Garage – look out for the brown tourist signs – you will see the Station on your right.

MID-SUFFOLK LIGHT RAILWAY MUSEUM

Address: Brockford Station, Wetheringsett, Suffolk IP14 5PW	**Nº of Steam Locos**: 2 (1 operational)
Telephone Nº: (01449) 766899	**Nº of Other Locos**: 1
Year Formed: 1990	**Nº of Members**: 400
Location of Line: Wetheringsett, Suffolk	**Annual Membership Fee**: £12.00
Length of Line: ¼ mile	**Approx Nº of Visitors P.A.**: 2,000
	Gauge: Standard
	Web site: www.mslr.org.uk

GENERAL INFORMATION

Nearest Mainline Station: Stowmarket
Nearest Bus Station: Ipswich
Car Parking: Available on site
Coach Parking: Available on site
Souvenir Shop(s): Yes
Food & Drinks: Yes

SPECIAL INFORMATION

The Mid-Suffolk Light Railway served the heart of the county for 50 years, despite being bankrupt before the first train ran. In a beautiful rural setting, the Museum seeks to preserve the memory of a unique branch line.

OPERATING INFORMATION

Opening Times: Sundays and Bank Holiday Mondays from Easter to the end of September and also on Wednesdays in August. Open from 11.00am to 5.00pm. Special events open at different times.
Steam Working: 2012 dates: 8th & 9th April; 6th & 7th May; 3rd, 4th, 5th & 17th June; 8th, 27th, 28th & 29th July; 5th, 10th, 12th, 19th, 24th, 26th & 27th August; 30th September; 28th October and 4th November. Please contact the railway or check the web site for further information.
Prices: Adult £6.00
Child £3.00
Family Ticket £15.00
Tickets allow unlimited travel on the day of issue and act as season tickets for the calendar year (subject to conditions).

Detailed Directions by Car:
The Museum is situated 14 miles north of Ipswich and 28 miles south of Norwich, just off the A140. Look for Mendlesham TV mast and then follow the brown tourist signs from the A140.

Midland Railway – Butterley

Address: Butterley Station, Ripley, Derbyshire DE5 3QZ
Telephone Nº: (01773) 747674
Year Formed: 1969
Location of Line: Butterley, near Ripley
Length of Line: Standard gauge 3½ miles, Narrow gauge 0.8 mile

Nº of Steam Locos: 25 (+30 Other Locos)
Nº of Members: 2,000
Annual Membership Fee: £16.00
Approx Nº of Visitors P.A.: 130,000
Gauge: Standard, various Narrow gauges and miniature
Web: www.midlandrailwaycentre.co.uk

GENERAL INFORMATION

Nearest Mainline Station: Alfreton (6 miles)
Nearest Bus Station: Bus stop outside Butterley Station.
Car Parking: Free parking at site – ample space
Coach Parking: Free parking at site
Souvenir Shop(s): Yes – at Butterley and Swanwick
Food & Drinks: Yes – both sites + bar on train

SPECIAL INFORMATION

The Centre is a unique project with a huge Museum development together with narrow gauge, miniature & model railways as well as a country park and farm park. Includes an Award-winning Victorian Railwayman's church and Princess Royal Class Locomotive Trust Depot.

OPERATING INFORMATION

Opening Times: Site is open daily throughout the year (except on Christmas Day and Boxing Day). Trains run daily during Easter, all School Holidays and from 21st July to 31st August. Also on most weekends throughout the year and Thursdays in December.
Steam Working: Weekends and bank holidays throughout the year and most days in the school holidays. Phone for further details. 'Day Out With Thomas' 2012 events: 7th June to 10th June; 4th to 7th August; 27th to 31st December.
Prices: Adults £9.50 Children £4.95
  Senior Citizens £9.95
  Family £23.00 (2 adults + 3 children)
Note: Some special events are more expensive.

Detailed Directions by Car:
From All Parts: From the M1 exit at Junction 28 and take the A38 towards Derby. The Centre is signposted at the junction with the B6179.

NATIONAL RAILWAY MUSEUM – YORK

Address: National Railway Museum, Leeman Road, York YO26 4XJ
Telephone Nº: 08448 153139
Year Formed: 1975
Location of Line: York
Length of Line: Short demonstration line

Nº of Steam Locos: 79
Nº of Other Locos: 37
Approx Nº of Visitors P.A.: 800,000
Web site: www.nrm.org.uk

GENERAL INFORMATION

Nearest Mainline Station: York (¼ mile)
Nearest Bus Station: York (¼ mile)
Car Parking: On site long stay car park
Coach Parking: On site – free to pre-booked groups
Souvenir Shop(s): Yes
Food & Drinks: Yes

SPECIAL INFORMATION

The Museum is the largest of its kind in the world, housing the Nation's collection of locomotives, carriages, uniforms, posters and an extensive photographic archive. Special events and exhibitions run throughout the year. The Museum is the home of the Mallard – the fastest steam locomotive in the world and Shinkansen, the only Bullet train outside of Japan.

OPERATING INFORMATION

Opening Times: Open daily 10.00am to 6.00pm (closed on 24th, 25th and 26th of December)
Steam Working: School holidays – please phone to confirm details
Prices: Free admission for all
(Excludes some Special events and Steam rides)
Please phone 08448 153139 for further details.

Detailed Directions by Car:
The Museum is located in the centre of York, just behind the Railway Station. It is clearly signposted from all approaches to York.

NENE VALLEY RAILWAY

Address: Wansford Station, Stibbington, Peterborough PE8 6LR	**Nº of Steam Locos**: 16
Telephone Nº: (01780) 784444 enquiries; (01780) 784404 talking timetable	**Nº of Other Locos**: 14
E-mail: nvrorg@nvr.org.uk	**Nº of Members**: 1,300
Year Formed: 1977	**Annual Membership Fee**: Adult £14.00; Child £7.00; Senior £11.00; Family £34.00
Location: Off A1 to west of Peterborough	**Approx Nº of Visitors P.A.**: 65,000
Length of Line: 7½ miles	**Gauge**: Standard
	Web site: www.nvr.org.uk

GENERAL INFORMATION

Nearest Mainline Station: Peterborough (¾ mile)
Nearest Bus Station: Peterborough (Queensgate – ¾ mile)
Car Parking: Free parking at Wansford & Orton Mere
Coach Parking: Free coach parking at Wansford
Souvenir Shop(s): Yes
Food & Drinks: Yes

SPECIAL INFORMATION

The railway is truly international in flavour with British and Continental locomotives and rolling stock.

OPERATING INFORMATION

Opening Times: 2012 dates: Most weekends and Bank Holidays from March to the end of December. Also open on most Wednesdays from April to the end of September and at various other times. Santa Specials run in December. Please contact the Railway for further details. Trains run from 10.00am to as late as 5.00pm, depending on the time of the year.
Steam Working: Most services are steam hauled apart from on diesel days and times of high fire risk.
Prices: Adult £10.50 – £18.00
Child £5.00 – £9.00
Family £26.00 – £45.00 (2 adult + 3 child)
Senior Citizens/Disabled £7.50 – £14.00

Detailed Directions by Car:
The railway is situated off the southbound carriageway of the A1 between the A47 and A605 junctions – west of Peterborough and south of Stamford.

NORTH NORFOLK RAILWAY (THE POPPY LINE)

Address: Sheringham Station, Sheringham, Norfolk NR26 8RA **Telephone Nº**: (01263) 820800 **E-mail**: enquiries@nnrailway.co.uk **Year Formed**: 1975 **Location of Line**: Sheringham to Holt via Weybourne **Length of Line**: 5½ miles	**Nº of Steam Locos**: 4 (+ visiting locos) **Nº of Other Locos**: 4 **Nº of Members**: 1,800 (M&GNRS) **Annual Membership Fee**: £19.00 (Midland & Great Northern Railway Society) **Approx Nº of Visitors P.A.**: 150,000 **Gauge**: Standard **Web site**: www.nnrailway.co.uk

Photograph courtesy of Ben Boggis

GENERAL INFORMATION

Nearest Mainline Station: Sheringham (200 yards)
Nearest Bus Station: Outside the Station
Car Parking: Adjacent to Sheringham and Holt
Coach Parking: Adjacent to Sheringham and Holt
Souvenir Shop(s): At Sheringham Station
Food & Drinks: Yes – main catering facilities at Sheringham Station. Light refreshments elsewhere.

SPECIAL INFORMATION

Lunch and evening dinner trains are scheduled throughout the year. Please check the website for times and fares. Weybourne Station is licensed for weddings.

OPERATING INFORMATION

Opening Times: 2012 dates: Daily from 1st April to 4th November plus weekends in March and Santa Specials in December. Special Events: Vintage Transport Festival on 1st July; Beer Festival 13th to 15th July; Grand Steam Gala 31st August to 2nd September. Please contact the railway for information about further Special Event dates.
Steam Working: 9.45am to 4.30pm (high season)
Prices: Adult £10.50
Child £7.00 (Under 5s free of charge)
Family £35.00 (2 adults + 2 children)
Senior Citizens £9.50
Dogs and Bicycles £1.00 each
The prices shown above are for all-day hop-on, hop-off, Day Rover tickets.

Detailed Directions by Car:
Sheringham Station is situated just off the A149. Holt Station is located at High Kelling, just off the A148.

NORTH TYNESIDE STEAM RAILWAY

Address: Stephenson Railway Museum,
Middle Engine Lane, North Shields,
NE29 8DX
Telephone N°: (0191) 200-7146
Year Formed: 1986
Location: Stephenson Railway Museum
Length of Line: 1½ miles

N° of Steam Locos: 5
N° of Other Locos: 3
N° of Members: 30
Annual Membership Fee: £9.00
Approx N° of Visitors P.A.: 30,000
Gauge: Standard
Web site:
www.twmuseums.org.uk/stephenson

GENERAL INFORMATION

Nearest Mainline Station: Newcastle Central
(5 miles) or for the Metro Percy Main (1½ miles)
Nearest Bus Station: North Shields
Car Parking: Free parking available on site
Coach Parking: Free parking available on site
Souvenir Shop(s): Yes
Food & Drinks: Hot drinks machine available

SPECIAL INFORMATION

A programme of events and activities is available
from the Museum on request.

OPERATING INFORMATION

Opening Times: 2012 dates: Weekends and Bank
Holidays from 31st March to 4th November and
daily during School Holidays, 11.00am to 4.00pm.
Steam Working: Sundays and Bank Holiday
Mondays from June to September.
Prices: Adult Return £2.45
              Child Return £1.20
              Family Return £6.10
Note: Admission to the museum is free of charge.

Detailed Directions by Car:
The Railway is adjacent to the Silverlink Retail Park approximately ½ mile from the junction between the A19 and
A1058. From the A19/A1058 junction look for the signs for 'Silverlink' before following the Brown tourist signs
to the Stephenson Railway Museum.

NORTH YORKSHIRE MOORS RAILWAY

Address: Pickering Station, Pickering, North Yorkshire YO18 7AJ **Telephone N°:** (01751) 472508 (enquiries) **Year Formed:** 1967 **Location of Line:** Pickering to Grosmont via stations at Levisham and Goathland **Length of Line:** 18 miles **N° of Steam Locos:** 20	**N° of Other Locos:** 12 **N° of Members:** 8,000 **Annual Membership Fee:** Adult £18.00; Over 60s £14.00 **Approx N° of Visitors P.A.:** 330,000 **Gauge:** Standard **Web site:** www.nymr.co.uk **E-mail:** info@nymr.co.uk

GENERAL INFORMATION

Nearest Mainline Station: Grosmont (adjacent to the NYMR station) or Whitby
Nearest Bus Station: Pickering (½ mile)
Car Parking: Available at each station
Coach Parking: Available at Pickering & Grosmont
Souvenir Shop(s): Yes – at Pickering, Goathland, and Grosmont Stations plus Grosmont MPD
Food & Drinks: Pickering, Grosmont & Goathland

SPECIAL INFORMATION

The NYMR runs through the spectacular North York Moors National Park and is the most popular steam railway in the country. As seen in 'Heartbeat' and the first Harry Potter film. The railway now operates extended services to and from Whitby.

OPERATING INFORMATION

Opening Times: 2012 dates: Open on weekends in March then daily from 31st March to 4th November plus Santa Specials in December. Please contact the railway for further information.
Steam Working: Usually daily – please phone the Railway for timetable information
Prices: Adult Day Rover £17.00 – £22.50
Child Day Rover £8.50 – £11.30
Senior Citizen Day Rover £15.00 – £19.50
Family Day Rover Tickets £34.00 – £45.00
(2 adults and up to 4 children)
Note: The higher fares are for trips through to Whitby.

Detailed Directions by Car:
From the South: Follow the A64 past York to the Malton bypass then take the A169 to Pickering; From the North: Take A171 towards Whitby then follow the minor road through Egton to Grosmont.

NORTHAMPTON & LAMPORT RAILWAY

Address: Pitsford & Bramford Station, Pitsford Road, Chapel Brampton, Northampton NN6 8BA
Telephone Nº: (01604) 820327 (infoline)
Year Formed: 1983 (became operational in November 1995)
Length of Line: 1½ miles at present

Nº of Steam Locos: 6   **Nº Other Locos**: 6
Nº of Members: 350
Annual Membership Fee: Adult £12.00 and Senior Citizen £6.00
Approx Nº of Visitors P.A.: 9,300
Gauge: Standard
Web site: www.nlr.org.uk

GENERAL INFORMATION

Nearest Mainline Station: Northampton (5 miles)
Nearest Bus Station: Northampton (5 miles)
Car Parking: Free parking at site
Coach Parking: Free parking at site
Souvenir Shop(s): Yes
Food & Drinks: Yes

SPECIAL INFORMATION

The railway operates on a section of the old London & North Western Railway line between Northampton and Market Harborough and became operational again on 18th November 1995. Work is currently underway on a southern extension to the line and the N&LR hope to open this in 2013.

OPERATING INFORMATION

Opening Times: Sundays and Bank holidays from March until the end of October and Santa Specials in December. Open from 10.30am to 4.30pm (the last train runs at 3.30pm). Please contact the railway for a more detailed timetable.
Steam Working: Bank Holiday weekends and Santa Specials in December. Steam and Diesel trains run on alternating Sundays during other times. Please contact the railway for further information.
Prices: Adult £4.60
Child £3.60 (Under-2s ride free)
Family £14.50 (2 adults + 2 children)
Senior Citizen £3.60
Fares may vary on Special Event days.

Detailed Directions by Car:
The station is situated along the Pitsford road at Chapel Brampton, approximately 5 miles north of Northampton. Heading north out of town, it is signposted to the right on the A5199 (A50) Welford Road at Chapel Brampton crossroads or on the left on the A508 Market Harborough road at the Pitsford turn.

NORTHANTS. IRONSTONE RAILWAY TRUST

Address: Hunsbury Hill Museum, Hunsbury Hill Country Park, West Hunsbury, Northampton NN4 9UW	**Nº of Steam Locos**: 3
Telephone Nº: (01604) 702031	**Nº of Other Locos**: 4
Year Formed: 1974	**Nº of Members**: Approximately 60
Location of Line: Hunsbury Hill Country Park, Northampton	**Annual Membership Fee**: £10.00 Adult
	Approx Nº of Visitors P.A.: Not known
	Gauge: Standard
Length of Line: Two-thirds of a mile	**Web site**: www.nirt.co.uk

GENERAL INFORMATION

Nearest Mainline Station: Northampton (2½ miles)
Nearest Bus Station: Northampton (3 miles)
Car Parking: Large free car park at the site
Coach Parking: Available at the site on request
Souvenir Shop(s): Yes
Food & Drinks: Yes

SPECIAL INFORMATION

The Railway has recently re-opened after a major rebuild and now operates along two-thirds of a mile of track. The Museum is dedicated to the Ironstone industry of Northamptonshire.

OPERATING INFORMATION

Opening Times: The museum is open during Easter weekend, Spring Bank Holiday weekend then the first Sunday of the month from June to October and also on other Bank Holidays throughout the year. Trains run at these times also. There may also be a number of special events throughout the year (including Santa Specials) – please contact the railway for further information.
Steam Working: An hourly service runs between 11.00am and 5.00pm.
Prices: Adult £3.00   Child £2.00
                Concessions £1.50
Admission to the museum and site is free of charge but donations are always welcome.

Detailed Directions by Car:
Exit the M1 at Junction 15A, and follow the road for approximately ½ mile. Turn left onto the A43 and after approximately 1 mile take the 3rd exit at the roundabout onto Danes Camp Way (A45). After ½ mile take the 4th exit at the roundabout onto Hunsbury Hill Road. Continue over two mini-roundabouts past the Rose & Claret Public House. The entrance to Hunsbury Hill Country Park for the railway is on the left.

PEAK RAIL PLC

Address: Matlock Station, Matlock, Derbyshire DE4 3NA
Telephone N°: (01629) 580381
Fax N°: (01629) 760645
Year Formed: 1975
Location: Matlock to Rowsley South
Length of Line: Approximately 4½ miles

N° of Steam Locos: 4 **Other Locos**: 20+
N° of Members: 1,700
Annual Adult Membership Fee: £16.00
Approx N° of Visitors P.A.: 70,000
Gauge: Standard
Web site: www.peakrail.co.uk
E-mail: peakrail@peakrail.co.uk

GENERAL INFO

Nearest Mainline Station: Matlock
Nearest Bus Station: Matlock
Car Parking: Paid car parking at Matlock Station. 200 free parking spaces available at Rowsley South Station and 20 free spaces at Darley Dale Station
Coach Parking: Free parking at Rowsley South
Souvenir Shop(s): Yes
Food & Drinks: Yes – R.M.B. Buffet on the train and the Rowsley Buffet at Rowsley South Station.

SPECIAL INFO

The Palatine Restaurant Car is available whilst travelling on the train and caters for Sunday Lunches, Teas and Party Bookings. Coach parties are welcomed when the railway is operating.

OPERATING INFO

Opening Times: Weekends and Bank Holidays throughout most of the year. Also Wednesdays from May to August, Tuesdays from late July to early September and some other dates. Santa Specials run during weekends in December. Please contact the railway for further information. Trains run from 11.15am to 4.20pm.
Steam Working: All services throughout the year.
Prices: Adult Return £7.50
             Children – Under-3s Free
             Children – Ages 3-5 £2.00
             Children – Ages 6-15 £4.00
             Senior Citizen Return £6.00
             Family Ticket £23.00
                 (2 adults + 3 children)

Detailed Directions by Car:
Exit the M1 at Junctions 28, 29 or 30 and follow signs towards Matlock. From North and South take A6 direct to Matlock. From Stoke-on-Trent, take the A52 to Ashbourne, then the A5035 to Matlock. Upon reaching Matlock follow the brown tourist signs.

PLYM VALLEY RAILWAY

Address: Marsh Mills Station, Coypool Road, Plympton, Plymouth PL7 4NW	**Nº of Steam Locos**: 4
Telephone Nº: (01752) 330881	**Nº of Other Locos**: 4
Year Formed: 1980	**Nº of Members**: 200
Location of Line: Marsh Mills to Lee Moor Crossing, Plympton	**Annual Membership Fee**: £10.00
	Approx Nº of Visitors P.A.: 5,000
Length of Line: ¾ mile	**Gauge**: Standard
	Web site: www.plymrail.co.uk

GENERAL INFORMATION

Nearest Mainline Station: Plymouth (4 miles)
Nearest Bus Station: Plymouth (3 miles)
Car Parking: Available on site
Coach Parking: Available on site
Souvenir Shop(s): Yes
Food & Drinks: Light snacks available

SPECIAL INFORMATION

The ultimate aim of the railway is to rebuild a 1¼ mile section of the ex-Great Western branch line which ran from Tavistock Junction, just outside of Plymouth, through to Launceston. The section to be rebuilt runs from Marsh Mills to Plym Bridge.

OPERATING INFORMATION

Opening Times: Open for static viewing on most Sundays from 11.00am to 5.00pm. 2012 operating dates: 8th & 22nd April; 13th & 27th May; 10th & 17th June; 8th & 22nd July; 12th, 26th & 27th August; 9th & 23rd September; 14th & 28th October and Santa Specials on 2nd, 9th, 16th & 23rd December. Also on 30th December. Trains run between 1.00pm to 4.00pm on all of these dates.
Steam Working: Most operating days. Please contact the railway for further details.
Prices: Adult Return £3.00
    Child Return £1.50
Note: There is no charge to visit the station.

Detailed Directions by Car:
Leave the A38 at the Marsh Mills turn-off and take the B3416 towards Plympton. Turn left into Coypool Road just after the McDonalds restaurant. From Plymouth City Centre, take the A374 to Marsh Mills, then as above.

PONTYPOOL & BLAENAVON RAILWAY

Address: 13a Broad Street, Blaenavon, Torfaen NP4 9ND	**Nº of Steam Locos**: 6
e-mail: info@pbrly.co.uk	**Nº of Other Locos**: 5 + 4 DMUs
Telephone Nº: (01495) 792263	**Nº of Members**: 350
Year Formed: 1980 (Opened 1983)	**Annual Membership Fee**: £14.00
Location of Line: Just off the B4248 between Blaenavon and Brynmawr	**Approx Nº of Visitors P.A.**: 12,700
	Gauge: Standard
Length of Line: 2 miles	**Web site**: www.pontypool-and-blaenavon.co.uk

GENERAL INFORMATION

Nearest Mainline Station: Abergavenny (5 miles)
Nearest Bus Station: Blaenavon Town (1½ miles) – regular bus service within ¼ mile (except Sundays)
Car Parking: Free parking for 50 cars on site
Coach Parking: Available on site
Souvenir Shop(s): Yes – at the Station and also a shop at 13 Broad Street, Blaenavon
Food & Drinks: Light refreshments on the train and at the station.

SPECIAL INFORMATION

The railway operates over very steep gradients, is run entirely by volunteers and is the highest standard gauge preserved railway in England and Wales.

OPERATING INFORMATION

Opening Times: 2012 dates: Every weekend and Bank Holiday Monday from 6th April to 23rd September. Also the second and fourth weekends of October, Wednesdays in August and Santa Specials on weekends in December. Please phone the Railway for details or check the web site for other dates.
Steam Working: Trains are steam-hauled during Peak days and special steam days. Diesel locos or DMUs may be used on quiet days. Please contact the Railway for further information.
Prices: Adult Return £6.00
　　　　　Child Return £3.50
　　　　　Family Return £15.50 (2 adult + 3 children)
Fares and conditions may vary for Special Events.

Detailed Directions by Car:
From All Parts: The railway is situated just off the B4248 between Blaenavon and Brynmawr and is well signposted as you approach Blaenavon. Use Junction 25A if using the M4 from the East, or Junction 26 from the West. Head for Pontypool. From the Midlands use the M50, A40 then A465 to Brynmawr. From North & West Wales consider using the 'Heads of the Valleys' A465 to Brynmawr. As you approach the Railway, look out for the Colliery water tower – you can't miss it!

RIBBLE STEAM RAILWAY

Address: Chain Caul Road, Preston, PR2 2PD	**N° of Steam Locos:** 24
Telephone N°: (01772) 728800	**N° of Other Locos:** 19
Year Formed: 2005	**N° of Members:** 400
Location: West of Preston City Centre	**Annual Membership Fee:** £15.00
Length of Line: 3 mile round trip	**Approx N° of Visitors P.A.:** 20,000+
	Gauge: Standard
	Web site: www.ribblesteam.org.uk

GENERAL INFORMATION

Nearest Mainline Station: Preston (2 miles)
Nearest Bus Station: Preston (2 miles)
Car Parking: Available on site
Coach Parking: Available on site
Souvenir Shop(s): Yes
Food & Drinks: Available

SPECIAL INFORMATION

The line traverses a swing bridge across the Marina entrance – the only preserved steam line in Britain to have such a feature! The railway also has the largest collection of standard gauge industrial locomotives housed under cover in the UK.

OPERATING INFORMATION

Opening Times: 2012 dates: Open 10.30am to 5.00pm on Sundays in April then weekends and Bank Holidays from May to 7th October. Also open on Wednesdays in August and for Santa specials on weekends in December. Please contact the railway for details of further operating days.

Steam Working: On all days when the railway is open to the public. Trains run hourly from 11.00am to 4.00pm.

Prices: Adult Return £5.50
Child Return £3.50
Family Return £15.00

Note: Prices may differ to those shown above.

Detailed Directions by Car:
From All Parts: The Railway is located on the Riversway/Docklands Business and Residential Park, just off the A583 Lytham/Blackpool road and approximately 1½ miles to the west of Preston City Centre. Follow the Brown Tourist signs from the A583 for the railway.

ROYAL DEESIDE RAILWAY

Address: Milton of Crathes, Crathes, Banchory AB31 5QH	**N⁰ of Steam Locos:** 1
Telephone N⁰: (01330) 844416	**N⁰ of Other Locos:** 2
E-mail: info@deeside-railway.co.uk	**N⁰ of Members:** 250
Year Formed: 1996	**Annual Membership Fee:** £15.00
Location of Line: Milton of Crathes	**Approx N⁰ of Visitors P.A.:** 3,000
Length of Line: 1 mile	**Gauge:** Standard
	Web site: www.deeside-railway.co.uk

GENERAL INFORMATION

Nearest Mainline Station: Aberdeen (14 miles)
Nearest Bus Station: Stagecoach Bluebird bus stop nearby on A93.
Car Parking: Free parking available on site
Coach Parking: Free parking available on site
Souvenir Shop(s): Yes – inside a static carriage
Food & Drinks: Yes – inside a static carriage

SPECIAL INFORMATION

The railway hopes to have the Andrew Barclay saddle tank "Bon-Accord" available for steam operation in late 2012 or early 2013. In the meantime, a guest steam loco will be operating on dates in 2012.

OPERATING INFORMATION

Opening Times: 2012 dates: Weekends from April to September and Wednesdays in July and early August plus some other dates. Also open for Santa Specials each weekend in December. Please contact the railway for further details.
Steam Working: 2012 dates: 1st, 7th, 8th, 9th, 21st & 22nd April; 5th, 6th, 12th, 13th & 27th May; 7th, 8th, 21st & 22nd July; 4th, 5th, 18th & 19th August and 29th & 30th September.
Prices: Adults £4.00 (£6.00 Steam days)
Children £2.00 (£3.00 Steam days)
Senior Citizens £2.50 (£4.00 Steam days)

Detailed Directions by Car:
From the South: Take the A90 to Stonehaven. Exit onto the B979 for Stonehaven and follow into the town square. Turn left at the traffic lights and follow signs for the A957 to Banchory (Historic Slug Road). Follow this road for 14 mile via Durris to Crathes and the junction with the A93. Turn left and follow the Brown Tourist signs, turning left for the railway after approximately 600 yards; From the North & West: Follow the A980 to Banchory and turn left onto the A93. Turn right following the Brown Tourist signs for the railway.

RUSHDEN TRANSPORT MUSEUM

Address: Rushden Station,
Station Approach, Rushden, NN10 0AW
Telephone Nº: (01933) 318988
Year Formed: 1985
Location of Line: Rushden, Northants.
Length of Line: ½ mile (each paid trip is 2½ miles in distance)

Nº of Steam Locos: 3
Nº of Other Locos: 4
Nº of Members: Approximately 600
Annual Membership Fee: £18.00 (Family)
Approx Nº of Visitors P.A.: 5,000
Gauge: Standard
Web site: www.rhts.co.uk

GENERAL INFORMATION

Nearest Mainline Station: Wellingborough (5 miles)
Nearest Bus Station: Northampton (14 miles)
Car Parking: Available on site. On operating days a nearby public car park must be used.
Coach Parking: None
Souvenir Shop(s): Yes
Food & Drinks: Available on operating weekends

SPECIAL INFORMATION

The Rushden Transport Museum is situated in the old Midland Railway Station of 1894 which once formed part of the Wellingborough to Higham Ferrers branch line. Taken over by the Rushden Historical Transport Society in 1984 the station also provides the society with a social club.

OPERATING INFORMATION

Opening Times: The Museum is open from Easter until the end of October on Saturdays (2.00pm to 4.00pm) and Sundays (10.00am to 4.00pm)
2012 operating dates: 17th & 18th March (Steam); 7th & 8th April (Steam); 19th & 20th May (Diesel); 3rd, 4th & 17th June (Steam); 30th June and 1st July (Diesel); 21st & 22nd July (Steam); 18th & 19th August (Mixed); 8th & 9th September (WD Shunter); 29th & 30th September (Steam); 20th & 21st October (Steam); 27th October (Diesel); Santa Specials on 8th & 9th December (Diesel) and 15th & 16th December (Steam).
Steam Working: See above
Prices: Admission to the museum is usually free but charges will be made on Special Event days.

Detailed Directions by Car:
From All Parts: Take the A6 to the Rushden Bypass (to the south of the A45) and turn into John Clark Way by the large grey warehouses. The Station is located on the right-hand side of the road after approximately 400 yards.

RUTLAND RAILWAY MUSEUM

Address: Cottesmore Iron Ore Mines Siding, Ashwell Road, Cottesmore, Oakham, Rutland LE15 7BX **Telephone N°**: (01572) 813203 **Year Formed**: 1979 **Location of Line**: Between the villages of Cottesmore and Ashwell **Length of Line**: ¾ mile	**N° of Steam Locos**: 13 **N° of Other Locos**: 13 **N° of Members**: 275 **Annual Membership Fee**: £10.00 **Approx N° of Visitors P.A.**: 8,000 **Gauge**: Standard **Web site**: www.rutlandrailwaymuseum.org.uk

GENERAL INFORMATION

Nearest Mainline Station: Oakham (4 miles)
Nearest Bus Station: Cottesmore/Ashwell (1½ miles)
Car Parking: Available at the site
Coach Parking: Limited space available
Souvenir Shop(s): On open days
Food & Drinks: On open days

SPECIAL INFORMATION

This Industrial Railway Heritage centre is located at the end of the former Ashwell-Cottesmore mineral branch and is based at the former exchange sidings. Major structural work is taking place and it is hoped that passenger services will resume during 2012.

OPERATING INFORMATION

Opening Times: Static viewing on Sundays from 11.00am to 4.00pm plus Tuesday and Thursday afternoons throughout the year.
Steam Working: Please contact the museum for further information.
Prices: Admission to the museum is free of charge (though donations are gratefully received). Charges will be made on Steam operating days and for other Special Events. However, no dates had been confirmed for 2012 at the time of going to press. Please contact the museum for further information.

Detailed Directions by Car:
From All Parts: The Museum is situated 4 miles north of Oakham between Ashwell and Cottesmore. Follow the brown tourist signs from the B668 Oakham to A1 road or the signs from the A606 Stamford to Oakham Road.

SCOTTISH INDUSTRIAL RAILWAY CENTRE

Address: Dunaskin Open Air Museum, Waterside, Patna, Ayrshire KA6 7JF	**Nº of Steam Locos**: 9
Telephone Nº: (01292) 313579 (Evenings & Weekends)	**Nº of Other Locos**: 15
	Nº of Members: 180
Year Formed: 1974	**Annual Membership Fee**: £12.50
Location of Line: Dunaskin Ironworks	**Approx Nº of Visitors P.A.**: 3,500
Length of Line: A third of a mile	**Gauge**: Standard
	Web site: www.arpg.org.uk

GENERAL INFORMATION

Nearest Mainline Station: Ayr (10 miles)
Nearest Bus Station: ½ hourly bus service from Ayr – phone (01292) 613500 for more information
Car Parking: Free parking available at the site
Coach Parking: Free parking available at the site
Souvenir Shop(s): Yes
Food & Drinks: Soft drinks and confectionery only

SPECIAL INFORMATION

The Railway is located at the former Dunaskin Heritage Centre which was unfortunately forced to close in 2006.

OPERATING INFORMATION

Opening Times: 2012 operating dates: 27th May; 3rd & 24th June; 1st, 8th, 15th, 22nd & 29th July; 5th, 12th, 19th & 26th August; 2nd and 23rd September. Please contact the railway or check the web site for further details.
Steam Working: On all operating dates.
Prices: Please contact the railway for further information.

Detailed Directions by Car:
From All Parts: Dunaskin Open Air Museum is located adjacent to the A713 Ayr to Castle Douglas road approximately 10 miles to the southwest of Ayr.

SEVERN VALLEY RAILWAY

Address: Railway Station, Bewdley,
Worcestershire   DY12 1BG
Telephone Nº: (01299) 403816
Year Formed: 1965
Location of Line: Kidderminster
(Worcs.) to Bridgnorth (Shropshire)
Length of Line: 16 miles

Nº of Steam Locos: 27
Nº of Other Locos: 12
Nº of Members: 13,000
Annual Membership Fee: Adult £18.00
Approx Nº of Passengers P.A.: 248,000
Gauge: Standard
Web site: www.svr.co.uk

GENERAL INFORMATION

Nearest Mainline Station: Kidderminster (adjacent)
Nearest Bus Station: Kidderminster (500 yards)
Car Parking: Large car park at Kidderminster.
Spaces also available at other stations.
Coach Parking: At Kidderminster
Souvenir Shop(s): At Kidderminster & Bridgnorth
Food & Drinks: On most trains. Also at Bewdley,
Bridgnorth, Kidderminster and The Engine House

SPECIAL INFORMATION

The SVR has numerous special events including an
Autumn Steam Gala, 1940's weekend, Classic Car &
Bike Day and visits by Santa! 'The Engine House', the
railway's visitor and education centre, is a further
attraction at Highley.

OPERATING INFORMATION

Opening Times: 2012 dates: Weekends throughout
the year. Also daily from 28th April to 7th October
and during local School Holidays. Santa Specials run
at weekends and on some other dates in December.
Please contact the railway for further details.
Steam Working: Train times vary depending on
timetable information. Phone for details.
Prices: Adult Day Rover £16.50
          Child Day Rover £8.50
          Senior Citizen Day Rover £15.00
Note: Entrance to The Engine House is included in
the above prices and upgrades to First Class travel
are also available.

Detailed Directions by Car:
For Kidderminster take M5 and exit Junction 3 or Junction 6. Follow the brown tourist signs for the railway;
From the South: Take the M40 then M42 to Junction 1 for the A448 from Bromsgrove to Kidderminster.

SNIBSTON COLLIERY RAILWAY

Address: Ashby Road, Coalville, LE67 3LN
Telephone Nº: (01530) 278444
Year Formed: 2001
Location of Line: Snibston Colliery
Length of Line: 1,100 yards

Nº of Steam Locos: 4
Nº of Other Locos: 2
Approx Nº of Visitors P.A.: 100,000
Gauge: Standard
Web site: www.snibston.com

GENERAL INFORMATION

Nearest Mainline Station: Loughborough (10 miles)
Nearest Bus Station: Loughborough (10 miles)
Car Parking: Available on site
Coach Parking: Available on site
Souvenir Shop(s): Yes
Food & Drinks: Available

SPECIAL INFORMATION

The Railway is located on the site of the former Snibston Colliery which also hosts an interactive museum, outside play areas, a Country Park and a nature reserve.

OPERATING INFORMATION

Opening Times: From November to March open on weekdays, 10.00am to 3.00pm and on weekends from 10.00am to 5.00pm. From April to October, Snibston is open daily from 10.00am to 5.00pm. Trains operate only on certain dates. Please contact the Museum for further information.

Steam Working: No usual steam operation. Please contact the Museum for further details.

Prices: Adults £7.50 (Train rides £1.65 extra)
Children £5.00 (Trains rides £1.05 extra)
Concessions £5.50 (Train rides £1.50 extra)
Family £21.00 (2+2) or £27.00 (2 + 3) (Train rides £4.00 extra)

Detailed Directions by Car:
From All Parts: Exit the A42 at the A511 (Coalville) exit and follow the signs for Snibston.

SOMERSET & DORSET RAILWAY TRUST MUSEUM

Address: The Railway Station, Washford, Somerset TA23 0PP	**Nº of Steam Locos**: 2
Telephone Nº: (01984) 640869	**Nº of Other Locos**: 1
Year Formed: 1966	**Nº of Members**: –
Location of Line: Washford Station	**Annual Membership Fee**: £18.00 (Adult)
Length of Line: Station sidings only	**Approx Nº of Visitors P.A.**: 3,000
	Gauge: Standard
	Web site: www.sdrt.org.uk

GENERAL INFORMATION

Nearest Mainline Station: Taunton (17 miles)
Nearest Bus Station: Taunton (17 miles)
Car Parking: Available on site
Coach Parking: None
Souvenir Shop(s): Yes
Food & Drinks: None

SPECIAL INFORMATION

The Museum of the Somerset & Dorset Railway Trust contains a mass of exhibits about and memorabilia of this much loved line. This includes a reconstruction of Midford signal box and carriages and wagons including some undergoing restoration.

OPERATING INFORMATION

Opening Times: A full list of opening dates had not been set at the time of going to press. Please check the Museum's web site or phone for further details.
Steam Working: Please contact the Museum or check the web site for further details.
Prices: Please contact the Museum for further information.

Detailed Directions by Car:
The Museum is located at the Railway Station in Washford Village on the A39 Bridgwater to Minehead road.

SOUTH DEVON RAILWAY

Address: Buckfastleigh Station, Buckfastleigh, Devon TQ11 0DZ	**N° of Steam Locos:** 13
Telephone N°: 0843 357-1420	**N° of Other Locos:** 10
Year Formed: 1969	**N° of Members:** 2,000
Location of Line: Totnes to Buckfastleigh via Staverton	**Annual Membership Fee:** £17.00
	Approx N° of Visitors P.A.: 112,000
	Gauge: Standard
Length of Line: 7 miles	**Web Site:** www.southdevonrailway.co.uk

GENERAL INFORMATION

Nearest Mainline Station: Totnes (¼ mile)
Nearest Bus Station: Totnes (½ mile), Buckfastleigh (Station Road)
Car Parking: Free parking at Buckfastleigh, Council/NR parking at Totnes
Coach Parking: As above
Souvenir Shop(s): Yes – at Buckfastleigh
Food & Drinks: Yes – at Buckfastleigh & on train

SPECIAL INFORMATION

The railway was opened in 1872 as the Totnes, Buckfastleigh & Ashburton Railway.

OPERATING INFORMATION

Opening Times: 2012 dates: Daily from 24th March to 4th November. Santa Specials also run in December. Please contact the railway for further details.
Steam Working: Almost all trains are steam hauled.
Prices: Adult Return £11.80 Child Return £6.80
Family Return £34.00
(2 adults + 2 children)
Senior Citizen Return £10.80
Note: Extra discounts are available for large groups.

E-mail: trains@southdevonrailway.org

Detailed Directions by Car:
Buckfastleigh is half way between Exeter and Plymouth on the A38 Devon Expressway. Totnes can be reached by taking the A385 from Paignton and Torquay. Brown tourist signs give directions for the railway.

SPA VALLEY RAILWAY

Address: West Station, Tunbridge Wells, Kent TN2 5QY	**N° of Steam Locos:** 9
Telephone N°: (01892) 537715	**N° of Other Locos:** 7
Year Formed: 1985	**N° of Members:** Approximately 850
Location of Line: Tunbridge Wells West to Groombridge and Eridge	**Annual Membership Fee:** £20.00
	Approx N° of Visitors P.A.: 36,000
Length: 5 miles	**Gauge:** Standard
	Web Site: www.spavalleyrailway.co.uk

GENERAL INFORMATION

Nearest Mainline Station: Eridge (cross-platform interchange with the mainline)
Nearest Bus Stop: Outside Sainsbury's (100yds)
Car Parking: Available in Tunbridge Wells nearby in Major Yorks Road, Union House & Linden Close
Coach Parking: Montacute Road (150 yards)
Souvenir Shop(s): Yes   **Food & Drinks:** Yes

SPECIAL INFORMATION

The Railway's Tunbridge Wells Terminus is in a historic and unique L.B. & S.C.R. engine shed. The extension to Eridge is now open at weekends and on public holidays and tickets inclusive of entry to Groombridge Place Gardens are also available.

OPERATING INFORMATION

Opening Times: 2012 dates: Weekends and Bank Holidays from 31st March to 4th November. Some weekdays during School Holidays and also Santa Specials during on weekends during December.
Steam Working: Most services are steam-hauled. Trains run from 10.15am to 5.30pm (10.50am to 3.30pm midweek and during low season).
Prices: Adult Return £10.00   Child Return £5.00
             Senior Citizen Return £9.00
             Family Return £26.00 (2 adult + 2 child)
Discounts are available for groups of 20 or more.
Fares vary on some special event days.
Fares allow unlimited travel on the day of issue except for special event days.

Detailed Directions by Car:
The Spa Valley Railway is in the southern part of Tunbridge Wells, 100 yards off the A26. Tunbridge Wells Station is adjacent to Sainsbury's and Homebase.   For Eridge Station (Satnav TN3 9LE), follow signs off the A26.

STEAM – MUSEUM OF THE GREAT WESTERN RAILWAY

<table>
<tr><td>Address: STEAM – Museum of the Great Western Railway, Kemble Drive, Swindon SN2 2TA
Telephone Nº: (01793) 466637
Year Formed: 2000</td><td>Nº of Steam Locos: 6
Nº of Other Locos: 1
Approx Nº of Visitors P.A.: 100,000
Web site: www.swindon.gov.uk/steam
E-mail: adminsteam@swindon.gov.uk</td></tr>
</table>

GENERAL INFORMATION

Nearest Mainline Station: Swindon (10 min. walk)
Nearest Bus Station: Swindon (10 minute walk)
Car Parking: Ample parking space available in the Outlet Centre (charges apply)
Coach Parking: Free parking on site and nearby
Souvenir Shop(s): Yes
Food & Drinks: Yes

SPECIAL INFORMATION

STEAM tells the story of the men and women who built the Great Western Railway.

OPERATING INFORMATION

Opening Times: Open daily all year round from 10.00am to 5.00pm (but from 11.00am to 4.00pm during the Winter months). Closed on 24th, 25th and 26th December and 1st January.
Steam Working: During some special events only – please contact the Museum for details.
Prices: Adult Tickets £6.40
 Child Tickets £4.25
 Family Tickets £17.00
 Senior Citizen Tickets £4.25
 Children under 3 are admitted free
Note: Season tickets are also available

Detailed Directions by Car:
Exit the M4 at Junction 16 and follow the brown tourist signs to 'Outlet Centre'. Similarly follow the brown signs from all other major routes.   From the Railway Station: STEAM is a short walk and is accessible through the pedestrian tunnel – entrance by Emlyn Square.

STRATHSPEY STEAM RAILWAY

Address: Aviemore Station, Dalfaber Road, Aviemore, Inverness-shire, PH22 1PY
Telephone Nº: (01479) 810725
Year Formed: 1971
Location of Line: Aviemore to Boat of Garten and Broomhill, Inverness-shire
Length of Line: 9½ miles at present

Nº of Steam Locos: 7
Nº of Other Locos: 10
Nº of Members: 850
Annual Membership Fee: £21.00
Approx Nº of Visitors P.A.: 56,000
Gauge: Standard
Web site: www.strathspeyrailway.co.uk

GENERAL INFORMATION

Nearest Mainline Station: Aviemore – Strathspey trains depart from Platform 3
Nearest Bus Station: Aviemore (adjacent)
Car Parking: Available at all stations
Coach Parking: Available at Aviemore and Broomhill stations
Souvenir Shop(s): Yes – at Aviemore and Boat of Garten Stations
Food & Drinks: Available on Steam trains only

SPECIAL INFORMATION

The railway featured in the BBC series 'Monarch of the Glen' and operates from Aviemore Station.

OPERATING INFORMATION

Opening Times: Daily in July and August, most days in April, May, June. Most days in September and October (but for Mondays and Tuesdays) and other dates in December. Please phone for details. Generally open from 9.30am to 4.30pm.
Steam Working: Most trains are steam-hauled but diesel power is used whenever necessary. Please phone the Railway for details.
Prices: Adult Return £11.50 (First Class £18.00)
Child Return £5.75 (First Class £5.75)
Family Return £29.00
(2 adults and up to 3 children)
Senior Citizen Return £10.00

Detailed Directions by Car:
For Aviemore Station from South: Take the A9 then B970 and turn left between the railway & river bridges. For Boat of Garten from North; Take the A9 then A938 to Carr Bridge, then B9153 and A95 and follow the signs; From North East: Take A95 to Boat of Garten or Broomhill (3½ miles South from Grantown-on-Spey.

SWANAGE RAILWAY

Address: Station House, Railway Station, Swanage, Dorset BH19 1HB	**Nº of Steam Locos:** 5
Telephone Nº: (01929) 425800	**Nº of Other Locos:** 4
Year Formed: 1976	**Nº of Members:** 4,200
Location of Line: Swanage to Norden	**Annual Membership Fee:** Adult £21.00; Senior Citizen £15.00; Family £42.00
Length of Line: 6 miles	**Approx Nº of Visitors P.A.:** 200,300 (exact figures for 2011)
Gauge: Standard	**Web site:** www.swanagerailway.co.uk

GENERAL INFORMATION

Nearest Mainline Station: Wareham (10 miles)
Nearest Bus Station: Swanage Station (adjacent)
Car Parking: Park & Ride at Norden. Public car parks in Swanage (5 minutes walk)
Coach Parking: Available at Norden
Souvenir Shop(s): Yes – at Swanage Station
Food & Drinks: Yes – buffet available on trains and also Swanage Station Buffet and at Norden.

SPECIAL INFORMATION

The railway runs along part of the route of the old Swanage to Wareham railway, opened in 1885.

OPERATING INFORMATION

Opening Times: Weekends from early March then daily from late March to October. Also open on some other dates throughout the year. Usually open from 9.30am to 5.00pm although trains may run later from May to September and evening services operate during some dates in the summer.
Steam Working: Most services are steam-hauled. Please check with the Railway for further details.
Prices: Adult Return £10.50
Child Return £7.00
Family Ticket £30.00

Detailed Directions by Car:
Norden Park & Ride Station is situated off the A351 on the approach to Corfe Castle. Swanage Station is situated in the centre of the town, just a few minutes walk from the beach. Take the A351 to reach Swanage.

Swindon & Cricklade Railway

Address: Blunsdon Station, Tadpole Lane, Blunsdon, Swindon, Wilts SN25 2DA	**N° of Steam Locos:** 6
Phone N°: (01793) 771615	**N° of Other Locos:** 8
Year Formed: 1978	**N° of Members:** 700
Location of Line: Blunsdon to Hayes Knoll	**Annual Membership Fee:** £14.00
Length of Line: 2½ miles	**Approx N° of Visitors P.A.:** 16,000
	Gauge: Standard

GENERAL INFORMATION

Nearest Mainline Station: Swindon (5 miles)
Nearest Bus Station: Bus stop at Oakhurst (¾ mile)
Car Parking: Free parking at Blunsdon Station
Coach Parking: Free parking at Blunsdon Station
Souvenir Shop(s): Yes
Food & Drinks: Yes

SPECIAL INFORMATION

The Engine Shed at Hayes Knoll Station is open to the public.

Web site: www.swindon-cricklade-railway.org

OPERATING INFORMATION

Opening Times: The Railway is open every weekend and Bank Holiday from February to December. Santa Specials run in December and other various special events throughout the year also have Steam train rides. Open 11.00am to 4.00pm.
Steam Working: Every Sunday from Easter until the end of October and certain other dates – please contact the railway for further details.
Prices: Adult £7.00   Child £5.00
               Concessions £6.00
               Family £20.00
Prices are different for special events.

Detailed Directions by Car:
From the M4: Exit the M4 at Junction 15 and follow the A419. Turn left towards Blunsdon Stadium and follow the signs for the Railway: From Cirencester: Follow the A419 to the top of Blunsdon Hill, then turn right and follow signs for Blundson Stadium.

TANAT VALLEY LIGHT RAILWAY

Address: Nant Mawr Visitor Centre, Nant Mayr Quarry, Lower Bowl, Nant Mawr, Oswestry SY10 9HW	**Nᵒ of Steam Locos**: None
Telephone Nᵒ: (01948) 781079	**Nᵒ of Other Locos**: 3
Year Formed: 2004	**Nᵒ of Members**: 100+
Location of Line: Nant Mawr Quarry	**Annual Membership Fee**: £10.00
Length of Line: One third of a mile	**Approx Nᵒ of Visitors P.A.**: 5,000+

Address: Nant Mawr Visitor Centre,
Nant Mayr Quarry, Lower Bowl,
Nant Mawr, Oswestry   SY10 9HW
Telephone Nᵒ: (01948) 781079
Year Formed: 2004
Location of Line: Nant Mawr Quarry
Length of Line: One third of a mile

Nᵒ of Steam Locos: None
Nᵒ of Other Locos: 3
Nᵒ of Members: 100+
Annual Membership Fee: £10.00
Approx Nᵒ of Visitors P.A.: 5,000+
Gauge: Standard
Web site: www.tvlr.co.uk

GENERAL INFORMATION

Nearest Mainline Station: Gobowen (5 miles)
Nearest Bus Station: Oswestry (5 miles)
Car Parking: Available on site
Coach Parking: None
Souvenir Shop(s): Yes
Food & Drinks: None

SPECIAL INFORMATION

Other attractions at the railway include Woodland Walks, a picnic area and a Nature Trail.

OPERATING INFORMATION

Opening Times: Most weekends from 10.00am to 4.00pm and at other times by prior arrangement. Please contact the railway for further information.
Steam Working: None at present. Static displays only.
Prices: No charge although donations are gratefully received. Footplate rides may be available on occasional dates in 2012. Please contact the railway for further information.

Detailed Directions by Car:
From All Parts: Take the A5 to the Oswestry bypass then follow the A483 signposted for Welshpool. At the Llynclys Crossroads, turn right onto the A495 and, after about 2 miles, turn right at Blodwell Bank then take the first left and an immediate right turn for the railway.

TANFIELD RAILWAY

Address: Marley Hill Engine Shed, Old Marley Hill, Gateshead, Tyne & Wear NE16 5ET	**Nº of Steam Locos**: 29 Standard, 2 Narrow
	Nº Other Locos: 12 Standard, 15 Narrow
	Nº of Members: 150
Telephone Nº: 0845 463-4938	**Annual Membership Fee**: £10.00 (Adult)
Year Formed: 1976	**Approx Nº of Visitors P.A.**: 40,000
Location of Line: Between Sunniside & East Tanfield, Co. Durham	**Gauge**: Standard and Narrow gauge
	Web site: www.tanfield-railway.co.uk
Length of Line: 3 miles	

GENERAL INFORMATION

Nearest Mainline Station: Newcastle-upon-Tyne (8 miles)
Nearest Bus St'n: Gateshead Interchange (6 miles)
Car Parking: Spaces for 150 cars at Andrews House and 100 spaces at East Tanfield
Coach Parking: Spaces for 6 or 7 coaches only
Souvenir Shop(s): Yes
Food & Drinks: Yes – light snacks only

SPECIAL INFORMATION

Tanfield Railway is the oldest existing railway in use – it was originally opened in 1725. It also runs beside The Causey Arch, the oldest railway bridge in the world.

OPERATING INFORMATION

Opening Times: Every Sunday & Bank Holiday Monday throughout the year. Also opens on Wednesdays & Thursdays in Summer school holidays. Santa Specials run in December.
Steam Working: Most trains are steam-hauled and run from 11.00am to 4.00pm (11.30am to 3.30pm in the Winter). Trains on Thursdays are diesel-hauled.
Prices: Adult £9.00
Child £5.00 (Under 5's travel free)
Senior Citizen £6.00
Family £23.00 (2 adults + 2 children)

Detailed Directions by Car:
Sunniside Station is off the A6076 Sunniside to Stanley road in Co. Durham. To reach the Railway, leave A1(M), follow signs for Beamish museum at Chester-le-Street then continue to Stanley and follow Tanfield Railway signs.

TELFORD STEAM RAILWAY

Address: The Old Loco Shed, Bridge Road, Horsehay, Telford, Shropshire
Telephone Enquiries: 07876 762790
Year Formed: 1976
Location: Horsehay & Dawley Station
Length of Line: ½ mile standard gauge, an eighth of a mile 2 foot narrow gauge

Nº of Steam Locos: 5
Nº of Other Locos: 12
Nº of Members: Approximately 220
Annual Membership Fee: £12.00
Approx Nº of Visitors P.A.: 10,000
Web site: www.telfordsteamrailway.co.uk

GENERAL INFORMATION

Nearest Mainline Station: Wellington or Telford Central
Nearest Bus Station: Dawley (1 mile)
Car Parking: Free parking at the site
Coach Parking: Free parking at the site
Souvenir Shop(s): 'Freight Stop Gift Shop'
Food & Drinks: 'The Furnaces' Tea Room

SPECIAL INFORMATION

Telford Steam Railway has both a Standard Gauge and Narrow Gauge line as well as Miniature and Model Railways. Major line extension works are currently underway.

OPERATING INFORMATION

Opening Times: Every Sunday and Bank Holiday between Easter and the end of September. Santa Specials run in December. Open 11.00am to 4.30pm.
Steam Working: 2 foot gauge on all operating days. Standard gauge on the last Sunday of the month, every Sunday in August and also on Bank Holidays.
Prices: Adult all day tickets £5.00
Child all day tickets £3.00
Family all day tickets £12.00
Note: Higher prices apply for special event days.

Detailed Directions by Car:
From All Parts: Exit the M54 at Junction 6, travel south along the A5223 then follow the brown tourist signs for the railway.

THE WEARDALE RAILWAY

Address: Stanhope Station, Stanhope, Bishop Auckland DL13 2YS	**N⁰ of Steam Locos:** 1
Telephone N⁰: (01388) 526203	**N⁰ of Other Locos:** 4 (including DMUs)
Year Formed: 1993	**N⁰ of Members:** 850
Location: Stanhope to Bishop Auckland, County Durham	**Approx N⁰ of Visitors P.A.:** 25,000
Length of Line: 16 miles at present	**Gauge:** Standard
	Web site: www.weardale-railway.org.uk

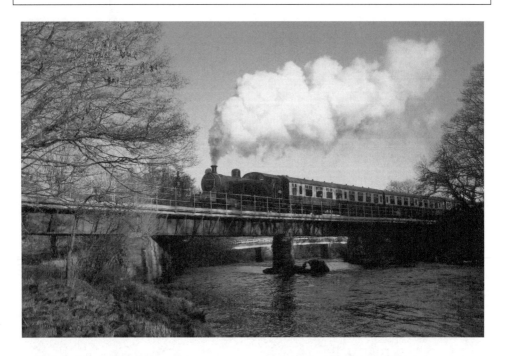

GENERAL INFORMATION

Nearest Mainline Station: Bishop Auckland (¼ mile)
Nearest Bus Station: Bishop Auckland
Car Parking: Available at both Stanhope and Wolsingham Stations
Coach Parking: Available at Wolsingham Station
Souvenir Shop(s): Yes
Food & Drinks: Yes – Signal Box Cafe, Stanhope

SPECIAL INFORMATION

Weardale is in the heart of the North Pennines and the railway provides magnificent unspoilt views. The area is known for its footpaths and bridleways and the railway provides a useful base for walks between stations along banks of the beautiful River Wear.

OPERATING INFORMATION

Opening Times: A heritage service operates between Bishop Auckland West and Stanhope on Saturdays and Sundays from Easter until the end of October plus Fridays during the Summer School Holidays. There are also a number of other special events throughout the year. Please contact the railway for further information.
Steam Working: No specific dates – trains may be Steam or diesel-hauled.
Prices: Please visit the railway's web site or contact Stanhope Station for further information. Tickets can be purchased on the train.

Detailed Directions by Car:
From All Parts: Stanhope Station is located in Stanhope, just off the A689; Bishop Auckland West Station is a short walk from the Northern Rail Mainline Station in Bishop Auckland (SatNavs use DL14 7TL).

WENSLEYDALE RAILWAY

Address: Leeming Bar Station, Leases Road, Leeming Bar, Northallerton DL7 9AR	**Nº of Steam Locos**: Visiting locos only
Telephone Nº: 08454 50 54 74	**Nº of Other Locos**: Various Diesel locos
Year Formed: The railway association was formed in 1990, the Railway PLC in 2000.	**Nº of Members**: 3,500
	Annual Membership Fee: £15.00
	Approx Nº of Visitors P.A.: Not known
Location of Line: Leeming Bar to Redmire	**Gauge**: Standard
Length of Line: Approximately 16 miles	**Web site**: www.wensleydalerailway.com

GENERAL INFORMATION

Nearest Mainline Station: Northallerton (7 miles)
Nearest Bus Station: Northallerton (7 miles)
Car & Coach Parking: Available at Leeming Bar, Leyburn and Redmire Stations
Souvenir Shop(s): Yes
Food & Drinks: At Leeming Bar & Leyburn stations.

SPECIAL INFORMATION

Most services are operated via DMU and travel to Leyburn & Redmire tourist destinations in the Wensleydale Valley. Other heritage diesel groups also use the line.

OPERATING INFORMATION

Opening Times: Weekends only during off-peak time plus other days over Christmas and New Year. Open daily during school holidays and most days (except Wednesdays & Thursdays) from 1st June to 30th September. Also other selected dates in October and November and Santa Specials in December.

Steam Working: Visiting steam locos will operate on some dates from 5th May to 23rd September 2012. Please contact the railway for further information.

Prices: Adult Return £12.50   Child Return £6.25
　　　　　Senior Citizen Return £11.00
　　　　　Family Day Rover £22.50 – £30.00

Note: Single and return tickets cost less depending on destination. Prices may differ during steam working.

Detailed Directions by Car:
From All Parts: Exit the A1 at the Leeming Bar exit and take the A684 towards Northallerton. The station is on the left after about ¼ mile close to the road junction and after the traffic lights.   By Bus: The Dales & District 73 bus route travels between Northallerton and Leeming Bar.

WEST SOMERSET RAILWAY

Address: The Railway Station, Minehead, Somerset TA24 5BG	**Nº of Steam Locos:** 7
	Nº of Other Locos: 12
Telephone Nº: (01643) 704996 (enquiries)	**Nº of Members:** 5,000
Year Formed: 1976	**Annual Membership Fee:** £17.00
Location of Line: Bishops Lydeard (near Taunton) to Minehead	**Approx Nº of Visitors P.A.:** 210,000
	Gauge: Standard
Length of Line: 19¾ miles	**Web site:** www.west-somerset-railway.co.uk

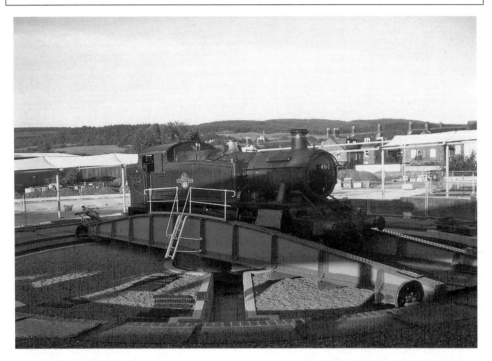

GENERAL INFORMATION

Nearest Mainline Station: Taunton (4 miles)
Nearest Bus Station: Taunton (4½ miles) – Service 28s run to Bishops Lydeard.
Car Parking: Free parking at Bishops Lydeard; Council car parking at Minehead and Watchet
Coach Parking: As above
Souvenir Shop(s): Yes – at Minehead, Bishops Lydeard and Washford
Food & Drinks: Yes – At some stations. Buffet cars on most trains.

SPECIAL INFORMATION

Britain's longest Standard gauge Heritage railway runs through the Quantock Hills and along the Bristol Channel Coast. The line passes through no fewer than ten Stations with museums at Washford and Blue Anchor and a turntable at Minehead.

OPERATING INFORMATION

Opening Times: 2012 dates: Various dates from February to December including daily from 12th April to 11th October. Open 9.30am to 5.30pm. Please contact the railway for more detailed dates.
Steam Working: All operating days except during Diesel Galas.
Prices: Adult Day Rover £15.60
Child Day Rover £7.80
Family Rover £43.00 (2 adult + 4 child)
Senior Citizen Day Rover £14.20

Detailed Directions by Car:
Exit the M5 at Taunton (Junction 25) and follow signs for A358 to Williton and then the A39 for Minehead. In Minehead, brown tourist signs give directions to the railway.

WHITWELL & REEPHAM RAILWAY

Address: Whitwell Road, Reepham,
Norfolk   NR10 4GA
Telephone Nº: (01603) 871694
Year Formed: 2009
Location of Line: Norfolk
Length of Line: Almost ½ mile

Nº of Steam Locos: 1
Nº of Other Locos: 1
Nº of Members: Approximately 400
Annual Membership Fee: £15.00
Approx Nº of Visitors P.A.: 6,000
Gauge: Standard
Web site: www.whitwellstation.com

GENERAL INFORMATION

Nearest Mainline Station: Norwich (15 miles)
Nearest Bus Station: Norwich (15 miles)
Car Parking: Available on site
Coach Parking: Available
Souvenir Shop(s): Yes
Food & Drinks: Available

SPECIAL INFORMATION

Whitwell & Reepham Station re-opened on the 28th
February 2009 nearly 50 years after it was closed to
passengers on 2nd March 1959. The intention is to
restore the Station to its former glory, re-laying of
track and sidings, acquiring rolling stock and setting
up a museum relating to the Station and The
Midland & Great Northern Railway.

OPERATING INFORMATION

Opening Times: Weekends throughout the year
from 10.00am until 5.00pm.
Steam Working: Usually the first Sunday each
month and also on Bank Holidays. Please contact
the Museum for further details.
Prices: Adults £2.00
Children £1.00
Family £5.00
Note: Prices shown above are for train rides –
admission to the museum is free of charge.

Detailed Directions by Car:
From All Parts: Take the A1067 Norwich to Fakenham Road to Bawdeswell then follow the B1145 to Reepham.
The railway is located about 1 mile to the South-west of Reepham and is well-signposted.

YEOVIL RAILWAY CENTRE

Address: Yeovil Junction Station, Stoford, Yeovil BA22 9UU	**Nº of Steam Locos:** 1 (2 from mid-2012)
Telephone Nº: (01935) 410420	**Nº of Other Locos:** 3
Year Formed: 1993	**Nº of Members:** 300
Location of Line: Yeovil Junction	**Annual Membership Fee:** £12.50
Length of Line: ¼ mile	**Approx Nº of Visitors P.A.:** 5,000
Gauge: Standard	**Web site:** www.yeovilrailway.freeservers.com

GENERAL INFORMATION

Nearest Mainline Station: Yeovil Junction (adjacent)
Nearest Bus Station: A regular bus service runs Monday to Saturday from Yeovil Bus Station (2 miles)
Car Parking: Available on site
Coach Parking: Available nearby
Souvenir Shop(s): Yes
Food & Drinks: Available

SPECIAL INFORMATION

The Visitor Centre is located in a GWR Transfer Shed which was built in 1864.
The centre also runs Driver Experience days.

OPERATING INFORMATION

Opening Times: Open regularly for Steam Train days, Mainline steam visits and other special events from March to October. Also open for Santa Specials in December and for static viewing every Sunday morning from 10.00am until noon. Please contact the Centre for further details of event days.
Steam Working: Numerous operating days throughout the summer. Please contact the Centre for further details.
Prices: Adult £6.00
Child £3.00 (Ages 5 to 15)
One child is admitted free with each paying adult
Note: Prices shown above are for Steam Working days.

Detailed Directions by Car:
The Centre is part of Yeovil Junction Station which is served by South West Trains. By road simply follow the signs to Yeovil Junction Station from Yeovil town centre or from the A37 Dorchester to Yeovil road. The entrance to Yeovil Railway Centre is through the low bridge, half way up the Yeovil Junction Station approach road.